ENIGMAS

Written by Vowery Dodd Carlile
Illustrated by Karen Birchak

ISBN 978-1-56644-369-2
© 2009 Educational Impressions, Inc., Hawthorne, NJ

EDUCATIONAL IMPRESSIONS, INC.
Hawthorne, NJ 07507

Printed in the United States of America.

TABLE OF CONTENTS

To the Teacher 4

Branches of Science 5

Scientific Method 6–7

General Questions about Enigmas 8

Stories, Discussion Questions and Creative Activities 11–87

   The Lost Civilization of Atlantis 11–20

   The Mystery of Stonehenge 21–29

   The Marfa Lights 30–38

   The Pyramids..39–48

   The Lost Colony of Roanoke Island 49–58

   The Loch Ness Monster 59–67

   The Bermuda Triangle 68–77

   The Nazca Lines 78–87

Learning-Activity Templates 88–89

Research Unit..91–109

Bibliography 110

To the Teacher

Students will have the opportunity to investigate, learn and create as they work through an enigma unit. They will also explore some of the many areas of science and how each approaches an enigma differently using the scientific process. A list of the branches of science and a description of the scientific method are provided. Students can refer back to these when answering certain questions at the end of their enigma story. This resource contains stories about eight enigmas. Each story is followed by discussion questions, creative questions, and learning-center activities that provide challenges for your gifted students as well as your on-level students. There is also a research unit which includes the steps to a successful research project and how to implement the unit.

Directions:

Step 1: Choose one of the enigma stories and read it together. Use the discussion questions at the end of the story to further students' understanding of the story. Duplicate and hand out pages six through eight to introduce or review the information about the branches of science and the scientific method. Then use the set of general questions to ensure that students understand what is meant by the term "enigma" and why the topic in the story just read is an example of an enigma.

Step 2: Students are now ready to complete the creative questions. These questions are asked at the upper levels of Bloom's Taxonomy and are designed to encourage students to think at a higher level and not just repeat information learned from the story. Many of the questions involve no right or wrong answers; therefore, grading will be subjective. Look for creative answers which have incorporated knowledge gained from the story.

Step 3: When the creative questions have been completed, assign or let students choose one or more learning-center activities. These activities include creative writing, illustrating, and/or the creation of a new product that will support the enigma story. They can be placed in a learning center for differentiation purposes or as extensions of the unit. A planning sheet and a template for creating additional learning-center activities are provided.

Step 4: When class participation following the reading of the chosen story is completed, students will choose another enigma story and begin their independent research project. The ability to conduct research on an assigned or chosen topic is a very important skill for future success in higher education. Directions are given in that section.

The objectives of this book are to encourage students to learn about enigmas, to use the acquired learning and to develop something new through a research project. In today's society, research is very important. The skills gained by completing this research will be used throughout their lives.

Branches of Science

What is science? Science is defined as the study of the world around us. It helps us answer questions about that world—questions such as *how?, what?, where?,* and *when?* Science also aids in finding solutions to problems that affect us and the world in which we live. There are many different branches of science. Below are some that might help in relating points of view about the enigmas in these stories.

PHYSICAL SCIENCE

Chemistry: the study of the composition, structure, properties and reactions of matter

Physics: the study of matter and energy and their interactions

Astronomy: the study of the matter and objects outside Earth's atmosphere

LIFE SCIENCE

Anatomy: the study of physical structures of animals, plants, and other organisms

Biology: the study of living organisms and how they interact with each other

Botany: the study of plant life

Ecology: the study of the relationships between organisms and their surroundings

Zoology: the study of animals

EARTH SCIENCE

Geology: the study of the origin, history, and structure of the earth and processes that shape the earth (or the solid matter of another celestial body, such as the moon)

Meteorology: the study of the atmosphere and its phenomena with a focus on weather processes and forecasting

Oceanography: the study of the ocean and everything in it, including land formations, water, and life

OTHERS

Archaeology: the study of ancient cultures through the examination of their material remains, such as buildings, graves, tools, and other artifacts usually dug up from the ground

Mathematics: the study of the relationships among numbers, shapes, and quantities

The Scientific Method

SCIENTIFIC TOOLS

Scientists use many skills in their search for answers. Some of these skills include the use of observation, identification, description, and inference.

Observation is a skill used to report what is seen, heard, smelled, touched, or tasted.

Description is the communication of what is learned by writing or telling about one's observations.

Identification is the recognition and naming of something.

Inference is a skill that uses previous knowledge and knowledge gained as a result of observation, description, and identification to draw conclusions.

SCIENTIFIC METHOD

The scientific method includes five steps that scientists use in their search for answers to unanswered questions or solutions to problems.

Step 1: State the problem. (What is the question of concern?)

Step 2: Collect information. (Research and gather information that will help you to understand the problem.)

Step 3: State the hypothesis. (Form a guess based upon the information.)

Step 4: Test the hypothesis. (Set up an experiment to prove or disprove the hypothesis.)

Step 5: Draw a conclusion. (Use the results of the experiment to reach a conclusion.)

The Scientific Method Record Sheet

State the Problem: _____

_____

_____

_____

Collect Information:

a._____

b._____

c._____

d._____

e._____

f._____

State the Hypothesis: _____

_____

_____

_____

_____

Test the Hypothesis: _____

_____

_____

_____

_____

Conclusion: _____

_____

_____

_____

_____

_____

_____

Enigmas: Discussion Questions

Before and During the Study of the Enigma

1. What is your understanding of an enigma?

2. Why does this particular enigma interest you?

3. What fields of science might be interested in this particular enigma?

4. How might scientists from the different scientific fields differ in their viewpoints about the enigma? Why?

5. How will an understanding of the enigma affect you? The world?

6. Have historical recordings of the enigma changed? Give examples.

After the Unit of Study

1. Has your viewpoint about the enigma changed? If so, explain your answer.

2. Did you experience any frustration when studying the enigma? If so, explain your answer.

3. What might you do differently if you studied another enigma?

4. Do you think it is important for scientists to continue their pursuit of answers to enigmas? Why or why not?

5. Can you think of a current enigma that might affect people in the future. Explain your answer.

ENIGMAS

THE LOST CIVILIZATION OF ATLANTIS

More than 2,300 years ago, the Greek philosopher Plato wrote of a thriving island continent that existed in the middle of the Atlantic Ocean more than 11,000 years ago. Whether or not this great civilization ever existed has been the subject of much debate. This civilization is known as Atlantis. The following is a fictional account of the destruction of Atlantis. It is based upon one theory of what might have happened.

Below the shadow of Mount Atlas lay the great city of Atlantis, surrounded by lush tropical-island foliage. On the hillside, whitewashed walls of grand villas with their red and orange tiled roofs glistening in the sun could be seen by sailors as they approached the harbor. The city was richly decorated with bronze statues and copper-lined walls. Atlantis was the home of the richest copper mines in the world. In fact, the Atlanteans were the only ones to mine, ship, and trade or sell this precious metal.

The land around the great city had fertile soil for farming or for grazing. Thick forests added to Atlantis's already rich economy. Hot, tepid, and cold springs dotted the island; some of those springs were converted into baths to be used by the aristocracy. Large palaces were built around some of the hot springs so the rich could leisurely bathe in the natural hot water that arose from the ground beneath the island. There were also public baths where everyone could experience the warm waters of the natural springs. All around the city, fountains of cold, clear water bubbled up from the ground, making it easy for those wishing to quench their thirst to get a drink.

Atlantis afforded those living on its lands a pleasant environment in which to work and in which to enjoy their leisure time. Many beautiful birds could be seen flying around the area. In fact, an abundance of wildlife was present; many of the animals were native to the island while others had been brought from faraway lands.

At the top of a central hill was a statue of Poseidon, god of the sea. Legend told of Poseidon falling in love with a mortal woman named Cleito. They married and she gave birth to five sets of twin boys, who later became the first rulers of Atlantis. The kingdom was divided among the brothers. Atlas, who was the eldest, became the first king of Atlantis. Poseidon loved Cleito so much that he created the hill on which his statue and temple were located to protect her. He surrounded the hill with rings of land and water. These sacred grounds on the hill provided a meeting place for the rulers of Atlantis to make laws, to think about and discuss important issues, and to pay tribute to Poseidon, one of their principal gods.

All seemed well in the paradise until small, seemingly unimportant, abnormalities began to take place. A silence slowly crept around the island. One would look for the birds and none could be seen. They had all flown from the land, in search of new homes. The rest of the wildlife on the island seemed uneasy. The race horses refused to run on the track and the goats, whose rich milk was enjoyed by everyone, stopped giving milk. The great elephants that were used to carry heavy loads of timber were unmanageable. The canals that led from the ocean into the harbor were full of dead fish. Some living on the island began to fear for their future.

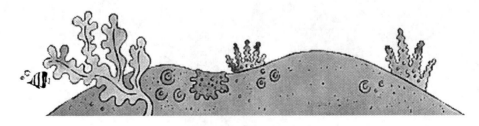

The priests who took care of the temples and made offerings to the gods were uneasy. They went to the emperor to speak to him about the many strange happenings, but he dismissed their warnings as unnecessary fears. One night the emperor and his family were having their meal in the garden. They sat in plush chairs. Their plates were made of finely sketched brass and placed upon an engraved wood table. Suddenly they heard a low rumbling sound and the ground began to shake. Fear appeared on the faces of the emperor's wife and children.

Many times the island had experienced rumblings from Mount Atlas. It was thought the gods were letting mortals know that they were watching over them, reminding the people of their strength. People paid little attention to the rumblings until that fateful day when Mount Atlas erupted. That day the shaking continued until great statues began to crumble and fall to the ground. Even Poseidon's temple fell in huge chunks, rolling down his sacred hill. People around the island ran in panic, trying to reach their boats that were tied in the harbor. Foul-smelling gases filled the air. Soon fire began to spout from the mountain. The fire was followed by giant boulders, which were sent crashing down the side of the mountain, smashing anything in their path. Hot lava began to flow down the mountainside as part of Mount Atlas exploded, leaving a large hole in its side. This was followed by a cloud of suffocating ash that covered everything it touched.

The screams of those trying to escape could be heard throughout the island. "Why have the gods forsaken us?" they shouted. Many small boats and ships made their way through the canals trying to reach the open waters of the sea. The people hoped they could escape the disaster happening before their eyes. The island was now a huge piece of land on fire. People in the boats watched in terror as their homes burned. Thinking they were safe, they thanked the gods for their safe escape.

But their relief was short lived. As they quickly rowed their boats and ships away from the island, they heard a noise. It began as a slight whisper but grew louder and louder until it became a roar, and they were met with a wave fifty feet high. Everything within its reach was sucked under into the depths of  its dark waters. And then there was silence. All those who had once called the great Atlantis home were gone—and so was the island itself!

THEORIES

Many have searched for this lost land of paradise, but as yet no one has found it. Some believe that Plato made up the entire story and that the civilization never existed. Others believe that it did exist. If so, what happened to such a great civilization that would cause its disappearance from the face of the earth? There are many theories that surround Atlantis.

- Plato, a Greek philosopher who lived from about 428 BCE to about 348 BCE, told of a great civilization that existed around 9000 BCE—a civilization that no longer existed. He described Atlantis as a very large island in the Atlantic Ocean just beyond the Pillars of Hercules (the Strait of Gibraltar)—more advanced, both socially and technologically, than other groups of same time period. Plato also claimed that Atlantis controlled most of the Mediterranean. Later Atlantis was defeated by ancestors of the Greeks, after which both civilizations disappeared.

- Some people believe that Plato made up the story as an allegory or to prove a point. They believe that Atlantis is a myth and never existed.

- Some think Atlantis was a continent that sank to the bottom of the ocean due to a natural disaster, such as an earthquake and/or a tsunami.

- Some think Plato might have based his account of the destruction of a great civilization upon the destruction of Helike, a city found on the shores of the Corinth Bay; the city was sunk by a massive earthquake. Today one can travel out into the Corinth Bay, look down into the water and see the remnants of Helike deep in the water.

- Some think that Atlantis was Crete because the Minoan Empire was destroyed by a tsunami. However, the time and location do not fit Plato's account.

- Some scientists think that Mount Atlas was a dormant volcano that came to life, destroying the island.

- A civilization similar to that of Atlantis was mentioned in historical documents found from other civilizations. For instance, Egyptian records describe an advanced civilization, its ruling family and a paradise environment; however, timing inconsistencies have created some doubt about this being the true Atlantis. Other cultures, such as the Mayas and the Aztecs, also mentioned the existence of a lost civilization using names such as Chilam Balam and Popol Vuh.

- A small minority believes Atlantis was created by aliens.

The Lost Civilization of Atlantis
DISCUSSION QUESTIONS

1. Describe the civilization of Atlantis using information from the story.

_____

_____

_____

2. Who was Poseidon and why was he important to Atlanteans?

_____

_____

_____

3. According to the story, what two natural happenings might have destroyed Atlantis?

_____

_____

_____

4. Who was Plato?

_____

_____

_____

5. How did Plato describe Atlantis?

_____

_____

_____

6. According to Plato, where was Atlantis located?

_____

_____

_____

7. Explain three possible theories about the destruction, creation, or existence of Atlantis.

_____

_____

_____

8. The story does not expressly say that a volcano destroyed Atlantis. What phrases can you use to infer that Mount Atlas was a volcano?

_____

_____

_____

9. What other cultures made note of the existence of a lost civilization?

_____

_____

_____

10. How has the lost civilization of Atlantis impacted our world?

_____

_____

_____

ANSWERS TO "THE LOST CIVILIZATION OF ATLANTIS" DISCUSSION QUESTIONS

1. *Describe the civilization of Atlantis using information from the story.* According to the story, Atlantis was a beautiful island with wildlife, fertile soil, and a rich economy that was based upon the mining, shipping and trade of copper as well as timber. It was a nice place to live with hot springs and fresh cool water that bubbled up from the ground.

2. *Who was Poseidon and why was he important to Atlanteans?* Poseidon was the god of sea. He was a principal god worshiped by the people of Atlantis. He would have been important to an island civilization.

3. *According to the story, what two natural happenings might have destroyed Atlantis?* According to the story a volcano and tsunami may have destroyed Atlantis.

4. *Who was Plato?* Plato was a Greek philosopher who lived from about 428 BCE to about 348 BCE. He wrote about a great civilization that existed around 9000 BCE—a civilization that no longer existed.

5. *How did Plato describe Atlantis?* Plato described Atlantis as a technologically advanced civilization that existed around 9000 BCE. He said that Atlantis controlled most of the Mediterranean but was eventually conquered by ancestors of the Greeks.

6. According to Plato, where was Atlantis located? It was located somewhere in the Atlantic Ocean just beyond the Pillars of Hercules, which we know to be the Strait of Gibraltar.

7. *Explain three possible theories about the destruction, creation or existence of Atlantis.* Some believe that Atlantis was destroyed by a volcano, a tsunami, or another natural disaster. Some believe that Plato made up the story to prove a point or to serve as an allegory. Some believe that Crete was the civilization referred to as Atlantis. A small minority thinks that aliens from another planet created the civilization.

8. *The story does not expressly say that a volcano destroyed Atlantis. What phrases can you use to infer that Mount Atlas was a volcano?* Phrases include the following: "Mount Atlas erupted," "foul-smelling gases," "fire began to spout from the mountain," "giant boulders…were sent crashing down the side of the mountain," "hot lava" and "a cloud of suffocating ash."

9. *What other cultures made note of the existence of a lost civilization?* Other cultures that mentioned Atlantis were Egyptian, Aztecs and the Mayas.

10. *How has the lost civilization of Atlantis impacted our world?* Answers may vary, but one possible thought might be that Atlantis has caused many scientists, explorers and treasure hunters to look for a civilization that was once one of the greatest in the world. Books have been written and movies have been created based on the subject. It has created a topic for entertainment.

The Lost Civilization of Atlantis
CREATIVE QUESTIONS

1. Several theories were mentioned in the story. Which do you think might have destroyed Atlantis? Give reasons to support your answer.

_____

_____

_____

2. Suppose you had been in Atlantis at the time of its destruction. What would you have done to try and save yourself and your family?

_____

_____

_____

3. Priests might have tried to warn the emperor that disaster was about to be inflicted upon Atlantis. How might you have convinced the emperor to evacuate the island?

_____

_____

_____

4. If you could change the story about Atlantis, what would you change and why?

_____

_____

_____

5. What else would you like to know to help you to make an educated guess as to whether or not the civilization existed and, if it did, the reason for its disappearance?

_____

_____

_____

6. Do you believe in the lost civilization of Atlantis? Give reasons for your answer.

_____

_____

_____

7. Suppose you were a scientist investigating the enigma of Atlantis. In which branch of science would you specialize and why? How would your viewpoint differ from that of another type of scientist?

_____

_____

_____

8. In your opinion, why did Plato chose to write about Atlantis?

_____

_____

_____

9. Suppose you were asked to choose three possible locations where Atlantis might have been found. Where would you suggest and why?

_____

_____

_____

10. Why, with the technology we have today, has the existence of Atlantis yet to be proved?

_____

_____

_____

Learning Center Activities
SUBJECT: The Lost Civilization of Atlantis

Name: _____

#1 Write a narrative about being present during the destruction of Atlantis.	**#2** Suppose you led an expedition that found proof of the existence of Atlantis. Write a newspaper article about your discovery. Include artifacts to support your findings.
#3 Research to learn more about the people who were supposed to have lived in Atlantis. Give an oral presentation to the class about your findings.	**#4** Create a board game based upon the lost civilization of Atlantis. Play the game with classmates. Have them rate its educational value from 1 to 10, with 10 being highest.
#5 Research the Greek philosopher Plato. Create a learning-center activity that will teach your classmates about Plato.	**#6** Choose one of the theories about the destruction of Atlantis and create a plan to test that theory.

Choose three activities to complete. As you complete each activity, record the date of completion.

Activity # _____ Completed _____

Activity # _____ Completed _____

Activity # _____ Completed _____

THE MYSTERY OF STONEHENGE

Imagine looking at a prehistoric monument that dates back about several thousand years. Stonehenge, located on the Salisbury Plain in southern England, is one of Britain's most valued ancient monuments. Its purpose is still unknown, yet all who have studied the great monument agree that regardless of the reason for its existence, it is an engineering marvel. Scientists think that Stonehenge was built in at least three different phases.

Phase I is thought to have been built by Stone Age man from around 2950 BCE to about 2900 BCE. (The exact dates of these phases differ. Some think Phase I was started around 2400–2200 BCE.) It began as a large circle dug into the ground using antlers from the red deer, oxen shoulder blades, and possibly wooden tools. Fragments of these tools were left in the bottom of the trench, which was 10 to 20 feet deep and 4.5 to 7 feet wide, by the diggers. These artifacts were identified and dated by archaeologists.

The initial circle was about 330 to 380 feet in diameter. The earth was removed from the trench and used to build an outside bank about 3 to 4 feet high. The inner bank, which was about 6 feet high and about 20 feet wide, was built from solid chalk that was found around the surface of Stonehenge. This bank measured about 320 feet in diameter. Just inside the circle 56 holes were dug and wooden posts were placed in the holes. These holes are known as the Aubrey holes, named after John Aubrey, who discovered them in the seventeenth century.

The entrance of Stonehenge faces the northeast and is about 35 feet wide. A huge stone, which has been named the heel stone, was set at the entrance. This made it possible for one standing in the center of Stonehenge to see a midsummer morning sunrise to the left of the heel stone. What is truly extraordinary is that the heel stone weighs 35 tons, is 20 feet tall, 8 feet wide, and 7 feet thick. Scientists question how people of the Stone Age had the capabilities to move the stone from its original location in Marlborough Downs, which is about 20 miles from Stonehenge. The heel stone is leaning, but most scientists think it had stood straight at one time.

About 12 feet from the heel stone is a covered ditch filled with chalk. Inside Stonehenge four more stones, called the Station Stones (only two still survive), were placed to form a rectangle perpendicular to the sunrise line of the heel stone. One Station Stone is naturally shaped while the others are somewhat tooled. There are some arguments about when the Station Stones were placed in Stonehenge, but most feel it was during Phase I.

Phase II is thought to have been built between 2900 and 2400 BCE. It involved the digging and placement of more posts in the center of the monument and towards the northeastern entryway. There did not seem to be any particular placement of the new lumber-filled holes. The original Aubrey holes were cleared of their posts and partially refilled with dirt; some were filled with cremation deposits. Over 50 holes containing cremation deposits were found, leading to the belief that Phase II was the earliest known cremation cemetery in the British Isles. Unburned bone fragments were also found in the outer ditch fill.

Phase III took place between 2550 and 1600 BCE. It seems that during this phase the builders replaced the timber with stones. Initially about 80 stones—the bluestones—were placed, but only 43 are still traceable today. Throughout this phase additional stones were brought in, some weighing 50 tons. Because there were no stones close to the Salisbury Plain, they had to have been brought from places about 20 to 30 miles away.

Stones were set in structure forms to hold other stones placed on top, eventually forming a circle. More were added, creating circles within circles. Other stones were placed to form a horseshoe shape. Changes continued to be made, with some stones taken away and others added. The entrance was also changed to make it possible for one to observe the midsummer sunrise taking place directly over the heel stone. Somewhere between 2600 and 2400 BCE a timber circle was constructed some 2 miles away from Stonehenge in an area that overlooked the Avon River. Some scholars believe that the timber circle was a symbol for "the land of the living" and the Avon River provided the path one takes during his or her lifetime, ending up at Stonehenge, "the land of the dead."

Carvings on some of the stones led archaeologists to think that some stones were added during the Bronze and Iron Ages. It is thought that the last construction that took place at Stonehenge was during the Iron Age. Roman coins and medieval artifacts were found around the monument; however, it is not known how Stonehenge was used during this time. Remnants of a seventh- or sixth-century BCE camp was found along the avenue close to the Avon. Also, the body of a seventh-century BCE Saxon man was unearthed in Stonehenge; this supports the belief that it may have been used as a burial ground during this time period.

THEORIES

Looking at the huge stones—some weighing as much as 50 tons—and thinking about their great weight, the distance the stones had to be moved, the manner in which they were placed, and the time periods in which these stones were transported and placed, one wonders how the tasks were accomplished. Many different experiments, using technology from the varied time periods, have been set-up in order to re-create the building of these massive structures. Although some of these have been successful, the exact means may never be known since there is not historical data to support the theories.

There are many unanswered questions about Stonehenge: Who built it? How was it built? Why was it built? Many theories have been brought out in an attempt to address these questions.

- Some of those mentioned as possibly being responsible for Stonehenge's existence are the Druids, the Greeks, Phoenicians, and the Atlanteans.

- A few believe that aliens from outer space or supernatural beings built the massive monument.

- It is widely believed that the first people to begin the construction of this great monument had no written language as no historical documentation has been found regarding Stonehenge's beginning.

- Possible reasons for Stonehenge vary. Some believe that it was used for the purpose of human sacrifices in religious ceremonies.

- Some believe Stonehenge was used as a place for healing.

- Evidence from recent archaeological studies proves that Stonehenge was used as a burial ground from its beginning.

- Many believe Stonehenge was used as a way to observe astronomical phenomena such as summer and winter solstices, lunar eclipses, and more.

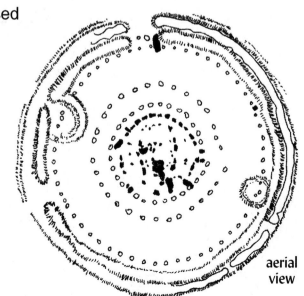

aerial view

These questions about Stonehenge may never be answered, but they do provide us with an exciting challenge to solve the mystery of Stonehenge.

The Mystery of Stonehenge
DISCUSSION QUESTIONS

1. What is the location of Stonehenge?

_____

_____

_____

2. When do scientists think Stonehenge was begun?

_____

_____

_____

3. When were Phases II and III thought to have taken place?

_____

_____

_____

4. What artifacts led archaeologists to think the first builders were of the Stone Age?

_____

_____

_____

5. Stonehenge was thought to have been built in three phases. Describe Phase I.

_____

_____

_____

6. When were the majority of stones most likely added to the monument?

_____

_____

_____

7. Give examples of two artifacts found at Stonehenge that help scientists to date it.

_____

_____

_____

8. What are two theories regarding the reason for Stonehenge?

_____

_____

_____

9. In which phase was Stonehenge's entrance changed and why?

_____

_____

_____

10. Explain how the timber ring, which was built to overlook the Avon River, was tied to Stonehenge?

_____

_____

_____

ANSWERS TO "THE MYSTERY OF STONEHENGE" DISCUSSION QUESTIONS

1. *What is the location of Stonehenge?* It is located on the Salisbury Plain in southern England.

2. *When do scientists think Stonehenge was begun?* They believe its construction began around 2950 to 2900 BCE.

3. *When were Phases II and III thought to have taken place?* Phase II was thought to have started around 2900 to 2400 BCE and Phase III from about 2550 to 1600 BCE.

4. *What artifacts led archaeologists to think the first builders were of the Stone Age?* Artifacts such as red deer antlers, oxen shoulder blades, and wooden tools were found; these artifacts were likely used to dig the ditch.

5. *Stonehenge was thought to have been built in three phases. Describe Phase I.* Phase I included the digging of a deep trench, circular in shape, with a bank on the outside and a higher bank on the inside. Eighty holes, which held timber posts, were dug around the inside of the circle. A huge stone, the heel stone, was placed at the entrance of the circle.

6. *When were the majority of stones most likely added to the monument?* Phase III shows the most amount of construction with the addition of stones.

7. *Give examples of two artifacts found at Stonehenge that help scientists to date it.* Cremation remains and sketched drawings of Bronze Age weapons on some of the stones helped to date Stonehenge.

8. *What are two theories regarding the reason for Stonehenge?* The following are some of the theories: a place for human sacrifices in religious ceremonies, a place for healing, a place to observe astronomical phenomena, and a burial ground.

9. *In which phase was Stonehenge's entrance changed and why?* The entrance was widened in Phase III so the midsummer morning sunrise would be directly over the heel stone.

10. *Explain how the timber ring, which was built to overlook the Avon River, was tied to Stonehenge?* Scholars think the timber ring was a symbol for "the land of the living" and that Stonehenge was "the land of the dead."

The Mystery of Stonehenge
CREATIVE QUESTIONS

1. Which theory about the reason for Stonehenge's existence do you support and why?

_____

_____

_____

2. How do you think the great stones were moved and placed at Stonehenge?

_____

_____

_____

3. Who do you think might have initially started Stonehenge?

_____

_____

_____

4. In your opinion, is Stonehenge is an exciting enigma? Explain.

_____

_____

_____

5. Suppose you were asked to research and answer one of the following questions about Stonehenge: Who built it? How was it built? Why was it built? Which would you want to answer and why?

_____

_____

_____

6. How do you think those who first built Stonehenge found out exactly where to place the heel stone so they could see the midsummer morning sunrise?

_____

_____

_____

7. Why, do you think, was Stonehenge constantly changed through the years?

_____

_____

_____

8. How do you think the Romans might have used Stonehenge?

_____

_____

_____

9. During Phase III a timber ring was built to symbolize the land of life. Compare this belief to your religious belief. How are they alike and how are they different?

_____

_____

_____

10. How might an archaeologist's viewpoint about Stonehenge differ from an astronomer's point of view?

_____

_____

_____

Learning Center Activities
SUBJECT: The Mystery of Stonehenge

Name: _____

#1
Design a travel brochure that would encourage tourists to visit Stonehenge.

#2
Write a fictional story using Stonehenge as its setting.

#3
Write a poem about Stonehenge including at least one theory as to the reason for its existence.

#4
Research the ways objects of great weight were moved in ancient times. Choose one and set up an experiment that would help explain how heavy objects were moved.

#5
Research a culture that might have been instrumental in designing and building part of Stonehenge. Present your findings to the class in an oral presentation.

#6
Use the scientific method to research one of these questions about Stonehenge: Who built it? How was it built? Why was it built? Present your findings in a journal.

Choose three activities to complete. As you complete each activity, record the date of completion.

Activity # _____   Completed _____

Activity # _____   Completed _____

Activity # _____   Completed _____

THE MARFA LIGHTS

On the outskirts of Big Bend National Park in West Texas lays the small, very ordinary town of Marfa. Located in one of the most sparsely populated regions of Texas, the area is home to many legends and unexplained happenings. What makes Marfa notable are the strange dancing lights that have been observed since the early eighteen hundreds. Marfa is the home to the greatest unexplainable mystery in Texas...the Marfa Lights.

Settlers, sheep herdsmen, cowboys and Native Americans from that region have reported seeing strange pulsating lights that appear to dance in the dark sky. The first recorded sighting of the Marfa Lights occurred in 1883 when cattleman Robert Ellison and his cowhands were driving cattle from Alpine through the Paisano Pass towards Ellison's ranch, which was about forty miles from Marfa. The men had bedded down the cattle for the night and were sitting around their campfires when they looked towards the Chinati Mountains and saw campfires. The fires seemed to be just a few miles away. Believing them to be Apache campfires and fearing that the Apaches would raid their herd, the cowboys quickly put out their own campfires and spent the rest of the night on the lookout for the Apaches. Nothing happened. The next day a few of the cowboys rode over to where they thought the fires were located and found no sign of Indians—no remains of campfires nor even tracks that might have been left behind. That night the same thing happened again. The cowboys saw the lights, investigated, and found nothing. The cowboys finally decided that the lights were not manmade and started calling them "ghost lights."

About 33 years later, Hallie Stillwell, a long-time resident who lived in Alpine and taught school in the neighboring town of Presidio, also saw the lights. Mrs. Stillwell reported that she first saw the lights in 1916 at the age of eighteen as she passed the Chinati Mountains while driving home from work late one evening. She stated that at the time she wondered whether Marfa would one day become famous for the mysterious lights. She said that at that time there were very few automobiles on the road, so she knew the lights were not from cars traveling on U.S. 67, a distant highway. Mrs. Stillwell recalled another instance when the lights flared up as a bright red, flickered, died down and then moved on to another place. She said that she had also seen the lights around the Cienega Mountains.

Seldom do the lights appear as one. If one light does appear, it quickly splits into two, three or four lights. The lights appear to remain suspended in mid-air and sometimes flicker like fire. They quickly move in odd directions, sometimes appearing to dance in the air. Some say that the lights are at first very bright but that they suddenly dim and then disappear.

The mysterious lights often change color and size. At times they appear to be bright white. At other times they appear greenish-yellow or a pastel shade. Some witnesses to the phenomenon have reported them to be bright red and blue. The size of the lights range from one to ten feet in diameter.

Although reports by those seeing the lights differ, there is little doubt of the famous Marfa Lights' existence. A viewing area has even been created nine miles east of Marfa along the outer edges of the old Marfa Army Air Field. Thousands of visitors, including scientists as well as sightseers, come to the area in hopes of being entertained by the Marfa Lights phenomenon. Over the years many experts from different branches of science have searched for an answer to the Marfa Lights. Several theories have been proposed, yet none have been proved. As the "old timers" from the area say, "Let 'em be." Perhaps it is an enigma that is not meant to be solved.

THEORIES

Many theories—from the scientific to the ridiculous, such as the idea that they are glowing jackrabbits or that they are the ghost of an Indian chief who was executed many years ago—have been proposed to explain the Marfa Lights. Several scientific theories should be noted. These include the following ideas:

- Some scientists feel that stars and planets appear close to the ground and are mistaken for the Marfa Lights.

- Some scientists feel that the strange movement of lights are caused by a type of mirage known as a Fata Morgana mirage. An upside-down image appears and the direct image seems to hover. Objects in the distance that are near the horizon appear elongated and elevated.

- Another theory is the Novaya Zemlya, which can best be described as light reflecting off several different layers of the earth's atmosphere rather than the normal two layers which divide warm and cold air.

- The theory of atmospheric tunneling has also been presented. This occurs when light is reflected from nearby objects and the reflections follow the contours of the earth. For example, reflections from the lights of automobiles that are traveling along a nearby highway become distorted by the atmosphere.

- Another theory involves triboluminescence. Friction on certain crystalline minerals, such as quartz, produces what appears to be a light. The area around Marfa is known to have an abundant supply of quartz.

- Ball lightning has been proposed by geologists as an explanation for the Marfa Lights. Normally lightning will strike in the form of a jagged line. There is, however, another rarer form of lightning that appears as a bright ball of light that moves quickly along objects or floats in the air. Although short lived, it appears for longer periods than normal lightning flashes. The cause of ball lightning is unsure, but it is thought be be ionized gas.

- An ophthalmologist theorized that the lights were simply an optical illusion caused by the eye's refraction. Because eye refraction is different for each individual, the Marfa Lights have appeared differently to those who have viewed them. However, this does not explain why the mirage occurs.

- Some say that pressure, due to stress and force on the tectonic plates in the earth's crust, causes the crust to react by producing the strange lights.

These theories are just a few explanations for the strange lights that appear east of Marfa, Texas. As with many other enigmas, the challenge of solving the phenomenon can be even more exciting than reading about it.

The Marfa Lights
DISCUSSION QUESTIONS

1. Where is Marfa located?

_____

_____

_____

2. Describe the earliest recorded sighting of the Marfa Lights.

_____

_____

_____

3. How did Mrs. Stillwell feel about the strange lights and their affects on Marfa?

_____

_____

_____

4. Why did Mrs. Stillwell dismiss the idea that lights came from automobiles?

_____

_____

_____

5. In what locations have sightings of the lights been reported?

_____

_____

_____

6. Describe the Marfa Lights as described in reported sightings.

_____

_____

_____

7. What is meant by a Fata Morgana mirage?

_____

_____

_____

8. How does the phenomenon known as triboluminescence relate to the Marfa lights?

_____

_____

_____

9. What might the tectonic plates have to do with the Marfa Lights?

_____

_____

_____

10. Define ball lightning. Have you ever seen it? If so tell about it.

_____

_____

_____

ANSWERS TO "THE MARFA LIGHTS" DISCUSSION QUESTIONS

1. *Where is Marfa located?* Marfa is located on the outskirts of Big Bend National Park in West Texas.

2. *Describe the earliest recorded sighting of the Marfa Lights.* The earliest recorded sighting took place on a cattle drive in 1883. The cowboys saw lights they thought were Apache campfires; however, no evidence of an Indian campsite was found.

3. *How did Mrs. Stillwell feel about the strange lights and their affects on Marfa?* Mrs. Stillwell wondered if the lights would make Marfa famous.

4. *Why did Mrs. Stillwell dismiss the idea that lights came from automobiles?* She did not think the lights were automobile headlights because there were few automobiles at that time.

5. *In what locations have sightings of the lights been reported?* The lights have appeared at the base of Paisano Pass, near the Chinati Mountains and around the Cienega Mountains.

6. *Describe the Marfa Lights as described in reported sightings.* The lights remain suspended in mid-air and sometimes flicker. They quickly move in odd directions, sometimes appearing to dance in the air. Sometimes the lights are at first very bright but then suddenly dim and disappear. The lights often change color and size. Sometimes they are bright white, sometimes greenish-yellow, sometimes pastel shade and sometimes bright red and blue. Their size varies from one to ten feet in diameter.

7. *What is meant by a Fata Morgana mirage?* An upside-down image appears and the direct image seems to hover. Objects in the distance that are near the horizon appear elongated and elevated.

8. *How does the phenomenon known as triboluminescence relate to the Marfa lights?* Friction on certain crystalline minerals, such as quartz, produces what appears to be a light. The area around Marfa is known to have an abundant supply of quartz. This could be what produces the images known as the Marfa lights.

9. *What might the tectonic plates have to do with the Marfa Lights?* Some believe that as the tectonic plates of the earth's crust move, stress resulting from the movement could create the strange lights.

10. *Define ball lightning. Have you ever seen it? If so tell about it.* Ball lightning is a rare form of lightning that appears as a bright ball of light that moves quickly along objects or floats in the air. Although short lived, it appears for longer periods than normal lightning flashes. The cause of ball lightning is unsure, but it is thought be be ionized gas.

The Marfa Lights
CREATIVE QUESTIONS

1. What might you do if you saw strange lights dancing around in the sky?

_____

_____

_____

2. Have you ever seen something strange that might be hard to identify? If so, tell about it.

_____

_____

_____

3. Suppose you had been one of the cowboys moving cattle and that you witnessed the dancing lights. What might you have thought? Remember that they did not have access to current technology as we do today.

_____

_____

_____

4. Which theory or theories do you think can easily be disqualified? Give reasons for your answer.

_____

_____

_____

5. In your opinion, who might be most interested in solving the mystery of the Marfa lights? Give reasons for your answer.

_____

_____

_____

6. Which theory would you like to test and why?

_____

_____

_____

7. What do you think prompted area residents to make the statement "Let 'em be" when discussing the Marfa Lights?

_____

_____

_____

8. Keeping in mind that the Apaches associated natural phenomena with supernatural powers, what might the Apaches have thought about the strange lights?

_____

_____

_____

9. Do you think the mystery of the Marfa Lights will ever be solved? Why or why not?

_____

_____

_____

10. Suppose the mysterious lights were space aliens. Why might they appear only at night?

_____

_____

_____

Learning Center Activities
SUBJECT: The Marfa Lights

Name: _____

#1
Locate Marfa and the areas in which sightings of the Marfa Lights have been reported. Point out these locations to the class.

#2
Write a poem about the Marfa Lights.

#3
Set up an experiment using lights and mirrors. See what distances reflections might occur. Can this have anything to do with the Marfa Lights? Write your findings.

#4
Write a story about the Marfa Lights. Chose one of the following: legend, science fiction, or mystery.

#5
Research the topic of atmospheric tunneling. Present your findings to the class.

#6
Choose one of the proposed theories and set up a method to test it. Use the scientific method. Record your findings.

Choose three activities to complete. As you complete each activity, record the date of completion.

Activity # _____   Completed _____

Activity # _____   Completed _____

Activity # _____   Completed _____

THE PYRAMIDS

The sounds of exhausted men, laboring tirelessly to build their god/leader, or pharaoh, a home for his afterlife, echoed through the dry desert area of Egypt. The time of building pyramids is long gone, but these great structures still remain today, some dating back almost 5,000 years. Eighty pyramids were built on the west bank of the Nile River. The reason the west bank was chosen was that the ancient Egyptians believed that the land of the dead was on the west side of the Nile.

Early pyramids were step pyramids. The step pyramid built for the pharaoh Zoser dates from about 2700 BCE. It is thought to be the oldest building left standing on Earth. The structure is very elaborate with six great, flat-roofed buildings built one upon the other. There were many rooms in the buildings, but no doors. The Egyptians believed their pharaoh's spirit could pass through walls and, therefore, did not need doors. The room that held the pharaoh's body and treasures lay eighty feet underground beneath the structure.

The tomb was opened in 1925 to reveal…emptiness. Nothing remained of the pharaoh's mummy but his foot. All the artifacts were missing. What happened to the mummy and the artifacts buried with it? Perhaps it will never be known. Were the pharaoh's mummy and other objects ever placed in the burial room of the tomb? Were they were hidden in another room somewhere else within the pyramid? Is it possible that the mummy was hidden in a secret place outside his pyramid in a place known only by a few so the body would be protected and the pharaoh could safely pass into the land of the dead?

Today known as the Great Pyramid of Giza, the pyramid built for Pharaoh Khufu was as tall as a 40-story building with each side being as long as seven city blocks. Beginning at about 2600 BCE, it took many thousands of farmers and slaves about thirty years to build. About two million stones, some of them weighing as much as fifty tons, were used to build this wondrous pyramid. The outside of the pyramid was then covered with white limestone so it glistened in the sun. The Great Pyramid of Giza was on the original list of the Seven Wonders of the Ancient World.

Archaeologists believe the pyramids were built to house the bodies of the great pharaohs. The ancient Egyptians believed the body must remain intact in order to pass on and live in the land of the dead. Therefore, the mummified body was placed in the tomb with his or her treasures. Included were all the supplies the pharaoh would need to live the same lifestyle that had been enjoyed while alive. The famous tomb of Tutankhamen—one of the few discovered that was left almost completely undisturbed—held what are thought to be clay pots of breads, fruits, and drinks as well as his bed, chairs, tables, and even games that would entertain him in the afterlife. That is why the pharaohs' tombs, some deeply imbedded within pyramids, have provided us with so much knowledge about the civilization of Ancient Egypt.

Many hours of planning went into the design of a pyramid and many more in the actual construction. The first thing that had to be accomplished was to locate a good, solid site on which to construct the pyramid. The ground had to be stable enough to hold millions of pounds of stone. Once a site was found, it had to be leveled. The workers dug canals and ran water through them, watching the water levels. When an area was too high, they used hammers and chisels to remove rock until the site was completely level.

Huge blocks of stone were cut and brought to the site. Most of the stones weighed about 2 1/2 tons, but some weighed much more than that! The stones were carefully laid in place, some so close that a knife could not be put between them. Of course, the inside of the pyramid was full of tunnels and fake passageways that were designed to trick robbers who might try and to steal the pharaoh's treasures. Deep within the pyramid or underground lay the most important part, the tomb where the pharaoh's body would be placed. The roof of this room would hold a slab of stone that might weigh 40 to 50 tons. Once the basic construction of the pyramid was completed, the outside walls were covered with limestone, which made it sparkle in the sunlight.

Although the Egyptians were the only builders of the true pyramids, other civilizations, such as the Aztecs and Mayas, built their own versions of pyramids. The Aztec pyramid temples were built about 2,000 years ago. They were designed with flat tops and there was a staircase on at least one side. Unlike the Egyptians, the Aztecs filled the inside of their pyramids with gravel or rubble. Some of their pyramids stood 27 stories tall with 247 steps from the bottom to the top.

The Mayas built thousands of pyramids. Most were constructed between the third and ninth centuries. Archaeologists think some of their pyramids are buried deep in the rainforest of Mexico and have yet to be discovered. Most of the Mayan pyramids had two or four staircases, which led from the ground to the temple, which was at the top of the pyramid. The priest-kings would climb to the top to perform sacrificial rituals. Some pyramids also served as burial places for important people.

One Mayan pyramid found deep in the rain forest of southern Mexico was in the ancient city of Chichen Itza. It had four staircases, three with 91 steps and one with 92. The total number of steps is 365, one for each day of the year. Chichen Itza is listed as one of the Seven Wonders of the World.

All agree that it took an amazing understanding of design and construction techniques to build structures 5,000 years ago that that can still be seen today. There are many questions left unanswered about these great structures. These questions present a challenge to scientists or to anyone else interested in solving the enigma of the pyramids.

THEORIES

The following are some theories regarding the building of the Egyptian pyramids.

- Engineers and architects have studied the pyramids in search of an answer as to how these great architectural feats were accomplished. Some think a ramp was built alongside the pyramid to move the heavy blocks of stone up to each level. Once the construction was completed, the ramp could have been disabled.

- It was once speculated that it took several hundred men to drag each stone into place. Later, the a Polish architect thought that 25 men could have dragged a block weighing 1 1/2 tons up to the pyramid; however, more modern tests have shown that if the surface was lubricated, then perhaps as few as 8 to 12 men could have pulled a block of stone up the ramp. Some physicists and mathematicians think that rather than needing hundreds of thousands of workers to build the pyramids, the jobs could have been done with as few as 10,000 men for the medium-sized pyramids and 36,000 for the largest.

- Archaeologists think the stone used for the structure may have been cut near the pyramid and rolled on great logs to their final destination. The limestone used for the outside of the pyramid was thought to be moved down the Nile River and over to the pyramid by way of human-built canals. The closest granite quarry was some 40 miles away, so these great slabs of stone are thought to have been brought to the sites by boat.

- Some believe that—in addition to slaves—farmers worked during those periods of time when the Nile flooded the region, thereby preventing them from cultivating their lands.

The pyramids have been and possibly will always be an enigma of science. As yet, no evidence has been uncovered to explain how these great structures were built.

The Pyramids
DISCUSSION QUESTIONS

1. What was the primary function of an Egyptian pyramid?

_____

_____

_____

2. What is meant by the Great Pyramid of Giza? Describe it.

_____

_____

_____

3. Why were the pyramids built on the west side of the Nile River?

_____

_____

_____

4. What do we call the process used to preserve the body? Why did the Egyptians want to preserve the body?

_____

_____

_____

5. Name some items that were buried with the mummy.

_____

_____

_____

6. How do archaeologists know what might have been buried with the mummy?

_____

_____

_____

7. What had to be done before the construction of an Egyptian pyramid was begun?

_____

_____

_____

8. How did the Aztec and Mayan pyramids differ from those of the ancient Egyptians?

_____

_____

_____

9. What is to be special about the stairs in the Mayan pyramid found in Chichen Itza?

_____

_____

_____

10. Explain the difference between early estimates of the number of men it took to move a 1 1/2-ton stone and recent estimates.

_____

_____

_____

ANSWERS TO "THE PYRAMIDS"
DISCUSSION QUESTIONS

1. *What was the primary function of an Egyptian pyramid?* The pyramids were built to house the bodies of the pharaohs. The ancient Egyptians believed the body must remain intact in order to pass on and live in the land of the dead. Therefore, the mummified body was placed in the tomb with his or her treasures. Included were all the supplies the pharaoh would need to live the same life that had been enjoyed while alive.

2. *What is meant by the Great Pyramid of Giza? Describe it.* The Great Pyramid of Giza is the one built for the Khufu. His pyramid was as tall as a 40-story building with each side being as long as seven city blocks. It took about two million stones, some weighing as much as fifty tons, to build his wondrous pyramid. The outside of the pyramid was then covered with white limestone so it glistened in the sun.

3. *Why were the pyramids built on the west side of the Nile River?* The Egyptians thought the land of the dead was located on the west side of the Nile River.

4. *What do we call the process used to preserve the body? Why did the Egyptians want to preserve the body?* The process is called mummification. The ancient Egyptians believed the body must remain intact in order to pass on and live in the land of the dead.

5. *Name some items that were buried with the mummy.* Some items buried with the mummy included food, beverages, furniture and means of entertainment.

6. *How do archaeologists know what might have been buried with the mummy?* Archaeologists know from artifacts that have been found. Especially helpful were artifacts found in the intact tomb of Tutankhamen.

7. *What had to be done before the construction of an Egyptian pyramid was begun?* A stable site had to be found. It then had to be leveled. Canals were filled with water and the levels watched. When the ground was too high, the water level showed the workers and they would chisel it down until all the ground was level. After all the ground was leveled, the stones could be brought in and set.

8. *How did the Aztec and Mayan pyramids differ from those of the ancient Egyptians?* The Aztec and Mayan pyramids were not true pyramids. They had steps; they served as places for sacrificial rituals; and they were filled with rubble.

9. *What is to be special about the stairs in the Mayan pyramid found in Chichen Itza?* Each side of the pyramid has a set of stairs, three with 91 steps and one with 92. There is a total of 365 steps, the number of days there are in a year.

10. *Explain the difference between early estimates of the number of men it took to move a 1 1/2-ton stone and recent estimates.* Early estimates were based on the need for 100's of men to move a stone block. Scientists think that with the use of lubrication as few as 8 to 12 men could have pulled a stone up the pyramid ramp.

The Pyramids
CREATIVE QUESTIONS

1. Why, do you think, did the Egyptians abandon the design of the step pyramid?

_____

_____

_____

2. What might have led to the Egyptians' belief that the land of the dead was located on the west side of the Nile River?

_____

_____

_____

3. What do you think happened to Zoser's mummy?

_____

_____

_____

4. In your opinion, why did most of the rooms in the pyramids lack doors?

_____

_____

_____

5. How long do you think it took to cut out one stone that was used to build a pyramid using a simple stone hammer and chisel? Add another variable, such as the number of men chiseling.

_____

_____

_____

6. What method besides the one discussed in the story might the Egyptians might have used to move the great blocks of granite forty miles from the quarry to the pyramid?

_____

_____

_____

7. Do you think there will ever be another Egyptian tomb discovered that is completely undisturbed? Explain your answer.

_____

_____

_____

8. Where do you think the Egyptians acquired the knowledge to design a pyramid? Give reasons to support your answer.

_____

_____

_____

9. How do you think the Aztecs and Mayas gained the knowledge needed to construct their great pyramid structures?

_____

_____

_____

10. Why, do you think, have the pyramids withstood time and still stand today? Give reasons to support your answer.

_____

_____

_____

Learning Center Activities
SUBJECT: The Pyramids

Name: _____

#1
Create a brochure to attract tourists to a newly discovered pyramid. Provide a map that will guide the visitors through the structure.

#2
Write a story about a day in the life of a pyramid builder. You may write it in story form or as entries in a journal.

#3
Pretend to be have a mummification business. Another group is trying to compete with you. Design a brochure that will attract business for your group.

#4
Recreate an Aztec or Mayan pyramid using sugar cubes.

#5
Research the Aztec or Mayan civilizations and give a presentation to the class about the uses for their pyramids.

#6
Research simple machines. Choose three and show how they might have been used during the construction of a pyramid.

Choose three activities to complete. As you complete each activity, record the date of completion.

Activity # _____   Completed _____

Activity # _____   Completed _____

Activity # _____   Completed _____

THE LOST COLONY OF ROANOKE ISLAND

The following story is a re-creation of Governor White's hunt for the lost colony. It is based upon historical documents.

The year was 1590 and Governor White was looking forward to seeing his daughter, his son-in-law, his granddaughter, and the rest of the group of colonists whom he had left behind three years earlier. White was leader of an expedition to colonize the area, but he had returned to England to get the badly needed supplies. He had planned to get back to the colony at Roanoke Island sooner, but the Spanish war and lack of financial backing had gotten in his way. But he was here now—within a few hours of seeing the 117 men, women, and children that he had left behind.

The region had first been explored for England by an expedition organized by Sir Walter Raleigh, although he himself was not there. Queen Elizabeth liked what she heard about the area and encouraged settlement there. The colony was named Virginia after Queen Elizabeth, who was known as the Virgin Queen.

The expedition led by White was the second attempt at a settlement on Roanoke Island. White thought back to first attempt at settlement, which had taken place in 1585. It had been organized by Sir Walter Raleigh and led by Ralph Lane. The expedition had gotten a late start, so the planting season was over by the time they arrived. Their supplies ran low, and to make matters worse Lane got into a fight with the neighboring Indian tribe and eventually killed the chief. The men were tired of being hungry and morale was low. They began to think the expedition was doomed until Sir Francis Drake stopped by to see how the settlement was doing. The men, including Lane, jumped at the chance to catch a ride back to England with Drake. About a week later a supply ship landed and found the settlement deserted. Fifteen men were left behind to protect the fort that Lane and his men had built.

White's mind wandered back to his own expedition. In 1587 he and 117 hopeful colonists had left England for Virginia Colony. They had been excited at the idea of building a life in a new land. When they arrived at Roanoke Island, they expected to be greeted by the fifteen men who had been left behind; however, no one met them.

White and the colonists made their way towards the fort with a fear that something had happened to the fifteen men left behind by the supply ship. They feared that the Indians had killed the men. Unfortunately, his theory was proven correct when they discovered the bones of one of the men. The discovery frightened the new colonists; however, they faced their fear with courage, anxious to start a new life in a new world. Their new home seemed to be a good place that, with proper care, would provide a stronghold for England.

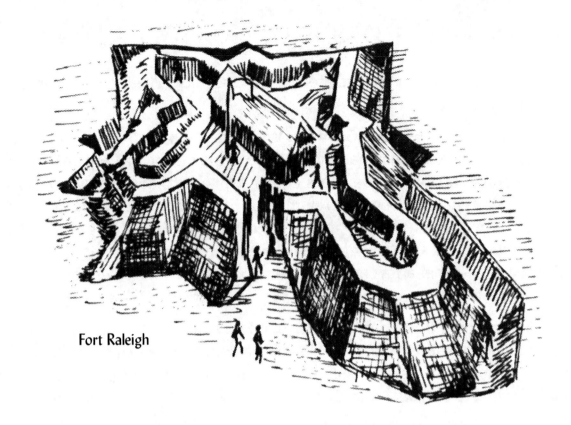

Fort Raleigh

It didn't take long, however, until Governor White realized the mistake that he made. He had incorrectly estimated the amount of supplies that would be needed to feed 117 people. He made the difficult decision to return to England for more supplies so that his expedition would not fail as the first expedition had.

Now—three years after he had left—White looked from the supply ship towards the shore. He had hoped to see at least some of the 117 colonists he had left behind lining up to welcome them, but no one appeared. It was getting dark, so plans were made to go to the settlement the next morning. Two boats—one to carry White and a few men and another for the captain and his crew—were dropped into the water.

The seas were rough! As the two boats made their way towards the shore, the captain's boat toppled over, drowning him and the six crew members who had accompanied him. White and his crew safely landed on shore. However, they had miscalculated the landing point about a mile, so White and his men had to hike to the settlement.

Once they arrived, there were no sounds to be heard. The fence that enclosed the fort was overgrown with wild bushes. They found the letters "CRO" carved into a tree and the word "CROATOAN" carved into one of the posts. However, the message did not have the Maltese cross or a distress sign, which White had instructed the settlers to use if they had to abandon the settlement.

Upon entering the fort, it was apparent to White and his men that it had been abandoned for quite some time. Large objects were thrown everywhere. The homes that once stood had completely disappeared. White searched for a chest that he had hidden. He found it with the contents dumped and scattered about. The chest had contained maps, books, and some personal belongings. The covers had been ripped from the books and the maps had been ruined by exposure to the weather. White's fear for the 117 men, women, and children that he had left behind grew.

The party searched the woods and the surrounding area for other signs of the colonists, but they found nothing. The weather began to turn stormy, so White and his men made their way to the boat so they could get back to the supply ship before the storm hit. White planned to sail to Croatoan Island. He hoped that the group had given up on him and joined the Croatoan Indian tribe there. However, the weather turned worse than expected and the ship had to return to England without an answer to the disappearance of the colonists.

Over the next several years, White tried to get back to Roanoke Island, but was never able to continue his search. The missing colony of Roanoke Island still remains a mystery today.

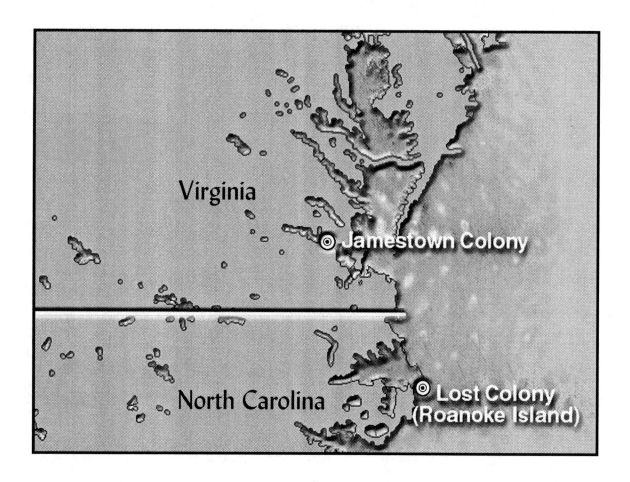

THEORIES

There have been many speculations as to the reason for the colonists' disappearance. Some of these are discussed below.

- Some think the colonists became tired of the struggle in that area and left the settlement. They believe the colonists may have moved to Chesapeake Bay and founded a new one; however, after exploring the area there was no evidence of a new settlement.

- Another popular theory was simply that the Indians in the area killed the colonists. Some people believe that Ralph Lane, the leader of the first expedition, had antagonized the Indians.

- Others have investigated the fact that the settlement was possibly destroyed by a storm. However, this does not explain why the fence around the settlement was left intact while the houses were destroyed.

- Some theories address the fact that the settlers joined a Native American tribe. They think that when times became too hard for them, they went to live with the native people.

- One theory states that the entire settlement died of disease; however, there were no bodies found anywhere.

No one has ever unraveled the enigma of the Lost Colony of Roanoke Island. The area is still being explored today by scientists looking for answers to the missing colony.

The Lost Colony of Roanoke Island
DISCUSSION QUESTIONS

1. Why was Governor White so anxious to get back to Roanoke Island?

_____

_____

_____

2. Why did the first expedition to Roanoke Island fail?

_____

_____

_____

3. Roanoke Island is located in present-day North Carolina. Where does the story lead you to believe Roanoke Island is located?

_____

_____

_____

4. Explain what happened when the supply ship landed after the first expedition.

_____

_____

_____

5. What happened to the men left behind to protect the fort?

_____

_____

_____

6. Why didn't White continue searching for the colonists?

_____

_____

_____

7. What puzzled White about the word carved into the post?

_____

_____

_____

8. What clues were found that caused White to think someone in the settlement had been violent?

_____

_____

_____

9. What hopeful thoughts did White have about the colonists' survival?

_____

_____

_____

10. What might have forced the colonists to leave the settlement?

_____

_____

_____

ANSWERS TO "THE LOST COLONY OF ROANOKE ISLAND" DISCUSSION QUESTIONS

1. *Why was Governor White so anxious to get back to Roanoke Island?* He had left the colonists there without supplies. He wanted to see his daughter, son-in-law, and grand-daughter.

2. *Why did the first expedition to Roanoke Island fail?* There was a shortage of supplies and Lane did not get along with the Native Americans in the region.

3. *Roanoke Island is located in present-day North Carolina. Where does the story lead you to believe Roanoke Island is located?* It is located somewhere in the present-day North Carolina. The story leads readers to believe it is located in Virginia because at the time of the story Roanoke Island was located in Virginia Colony.

4. *Explain what happened when the supply ship landed after the first expedition.* No one was at the settlement, so they left fifteen men to protect the fort until reinforcements came.

5. *What happened to the men left behind to protect the fort?* The fifteen men were thought to have been killed by the Indians.

6. *Why did it take White three years to return with the needed supplies?* The Spanish War and lack of financial support prevented White from returning sooner.

7. *What puzzled White about the word carved into the post?* White had instructed the settlers to leave a sign, such as a cross or distress sign, if they had to leave the settlement, but only the word "CROATOAN" was carved into the post.

8. *What clues were found that caused White to think someone in the settlement had been violent?* Things were thrown about, the houses had disappeared, his chest had been searched, and his personal things had been strewn about and damaged by exposure to the weather.

8. *What hopeful thoughts did White have about the colonists' survival?* White was hopeful that the group had given up on him and had joined the Croatoan Indian tribe that was on Croatoan Island.

10. *Why did it take White three years to return with the needed supplies?* The Spanish War and lack of financial support prevented White from returning sooner.

10. *What might have forced the colonists to leave the settlement?* Possible reasons are the lack of supplies, hopelessness for White's return, and hostile Indians.

The Lost Colony of Roanoke Island
CREATIVE QUESTIONS

1. Why, do you think, did England want to start a new colony on Roanoke Island?

_____

_____

_____

2. Had you been leader of the first expedition, what might you have done differently to assure its success?

_____

_____

_____

3. What do you think Governor White might have done differently to ensure the success of his expedition to Roanoke Island?

_____

_____

_____

4. What do you think was the significance of the word "CROATOAN" that was carved into the post?

_____

_____

_____

5. Several theories were proposed. Which one do you think explains the missing colonists best and why?

_____

_____

_____

6. Do you think it possible for disease to have killed everyone? Why or why not?

_____

_____

_____

7. If you had been one of the colonists, would you have chosen to live with the natives or would you have remained in the settlement and await White's return? Give reasons for your answer.

_____

_____

_____

8. Suppose you were a mathematician. How might you solve the Roanoke Island mystery?

_____

_____

_____

9. What other theory can you think of that might explain the missing colonists?

_____

_____

_____

10. What might you have done to encourage friendship with the native people?

_____

_____

_____

Learning Center Activities
SUBJECT: The Lost Colony of Roanoke Island

Name: _____

#1 Create a magazine advertisement that would attract people to settle on Roanoke Island.	**#2** Draw a map that depicts how a settlement might have looked in colonial times.
#3 Suppose you were responsible for gathering supplies for the 117 colonists to live through one year. Make a list of the supplies they might need.	**#4** Research colonial life and write a story about living in that time period.
#5 Research a task done by the colonists: making soap, cutting wood, building a house, planting & cultivating crops, etc. Write a guide on how to accomplish the task.	**#6** Using the scientific method, design an experiment to test one of the theories about the missing colonists of Roanoke Island.

Choose three activities to complete. As you complete each activity, record the date of completion.

Activity # _____   Completed _____

Activity # _____   Completed _____

Activity # _____   Completed _____

THE LOCH NESS MONSTER

Nicknamed Nessie, the so-called the Loch Ness Monster is said to inhabit Loch Ness, a deep lake located in northern Scotland. Loch Ness is the largest of all freshwater lakes in Great Britain and is one of several interlinking lochs, or lakes, that are found along the Great Glen.

The Great Glen is an area that runs through a large geological fault zone. There are always rumblings, spurts of energy that affect the loch water, and wave action in the lakes along the fault zone. Because the lake is very deep, dark, and murky and has underwater caves, it is thought to be a good hiding place for Nessie. Some scientists think the underwater caves once connected all the lakes and drained into the Moray Firth, which is now part of the Caledonian Canal.

Sightings of Nessie date back almost 1,500 years. Archaeologists have found evidence of those sightings in carvings done by ancient people of the Scottish Highlands. The carvings show a giant aquatic creature.

May 2, 1933, was the date on which Nessie joined the more modern world. Mr. and Mrs. John Mackay reported to a newspaper, the *Inverness Courier,* that they had seen "an enormous animal rolling and plunging on the surface" of Loch Ness. They described the animal as a monster about 40 to 50 feet long with two humps, a tail, and a snakelike head. A reward of 20,000 pounds (English money) was offered for the capture of creature.

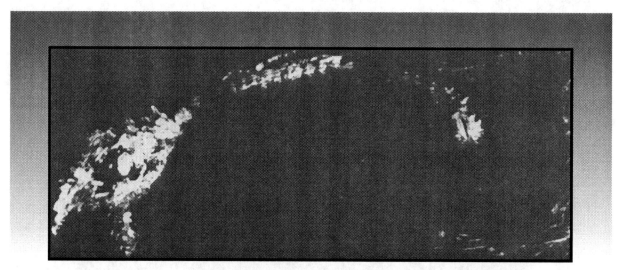

Artist's rendering of a 1975 Loch Ness photograph taken by Charles W. Wyckoff which was enhanced by computer at the Jet Propulsion Lab in California to better define object outlines. The photo seems to show the head and neck of a large aquatic animal.

Since then there have been many reported sightings of Nessie. Most of them record the Loch Ness Monster as having a long neck and a small head. It is usually said to have flippers that help it move quickly through the water. Some who claim to have seen the monster say it has a V-shaped mouth between twelve and eighteen inches wide. Others have described different details about Nessie's appearance. Regardless of Nessie's alleged appearance, the sightings have caused quite a stir in the region. Nessie sightings have turned tourism into a multi-million dollar business. Many hotels, restaurants, boat tours and Nessie souvenir shops have provided jobs for residents in the area.

There have been many pictures taken of Nessie. Some appear to be real, while others are obviously fake. One example of a fake photograph was produced by Marmaduke Wetherell, who was a big-game hunter. Wetherell was angry at the locals because some of the children had tricked him into thinking there really was a monster swimming in the loch. He began searching for the monster. He wanted to add it to his many other animal trophies; however, when the trick was revealed, he was laughed at by everyone. Wanting to redeem his name, he convinced his son-in-law, Chris Spurling, to create a fake picture of the Loch Ness Monster. Spurling used clay to form a monster with a hump back, a long neck, and a small head. The fake Nessie was then placed in water and photographs were taken that made it appear to be swimming in Loch Ness. Later his son-in-law—on his death bed—confessed to the photograph being a hoax.

Other photographs, however, seem to have some credibility. For instance, some scientists used sonar and underwater cameras equipped with high-powered lights to try to capture the creature photographically. The high-powered lights were necessary because the deep waters are so dark. Their photographs revealed an animal resembling a plesiosaur. The closer photos also showed what seemed to be diamond-shaped fins in different positions. The photos of the fins showed that there was movement of the animal.

These and other photos taken of what is thought to be Nessie seem to prove there is something present in the lake. Still, there remains a lot of skepticism as to the Loch Ness Monster's existence. Those who truly believe in Nessie continue to search for answers to the mystery of the Loch Ness Monster.

THEORIES

Many people believe in the existence of a prehistoric-type creature living in Loch Ness. However, there are many skeptics. The following are some theories about Nessie's existence.

- Some think that Nessie is a plesiosaur. Plesiosaurs were prehistoric reptiles that existed about 160 million years ago, becoming extinct around 65 million years ago. After studying fossils of the plesiosaur, scientists found that the bones in its neck were not strong and could not support holding its head up high in the water. They think it ate soft-bodied animals that lived on the sea floor. However, if Nessie were a plesiosaur, there would be more sightings because as a reptile it would need to come to the surface frequently to breathe.

- If Nessie does exist, there must be more than one since reports of sightings date back 1,500 years! Could the Loch Ness Monster be 1,500 years old? Zoologists think it would take at least ten Nessies to keep the species alive; however, they do not feel that the loch is large enough to support a small family of the creature.

- Nessie could just be a very large fish. Some zoologists think that Nessie is probably a Baltic sturgeon, a primitive fish that can grow up to 9 feet in length and can weigh as much as 450 pounds! It has a snout and spines that run down its back.

- Could Nessie be just an underwater wave? Geologists think that seismic rumblings can cause rolling waves which can create an explosive blast. When seen, the underwater wave might resemble a monster emerging from the water.

- Some scientists feel the lakes were connected by underwater caves that drained into the Moray Firth, which is part of the Caledonian Canal. This could be a possible way in which Nessie became trapped in Loch Ness when the underwater cave system collapsed.

- Some people believe that stories about Nessie are spread in order to attract visitors to the area to help the economy of the region.

Could there really be a monster-like creature that exists in the deep waters of Loch Ness? The question has yet to be answered. The challenge is to look for answers that scientifically support Nessie's existence.

The Loch Ness Monster
DISCUSSION QUESTIONS

1. What is the location of Loch Ness?

_____

_____

_____

2. Explain why some say that the Loch Ness Monster sightings date back at least 1,500 years.

_____

_____

_____

3. Describe the reported sighting of Nessie in 1933.

_____

_____

_____

4. How have sightings of Nessie helped the area?

_____

_____

_____

5. Tell about the fake photograph that was circulated of Nessie.

_____

_____

_____

6. How were the credible photographs taken?

_____

_____

_____

7. What do some scientists say about Nessie being a plesiosaur?

_____

_____

_____

8. Why do some think Nessie might be an underwater wave?

_____

_____

_____

9. Explain the importance of the fact that at one time all the lakes in the area might have been connected?

_____

_____

_____

10. According to some zoologists, what animal might be a possible explanation for Nessie?

_____

_____

_____

ANSWERS TO "THE LOCH NESS MONSTER" DISCUSSION QUESTIONS

1. *What is the location of Loch Ness?* Loch Ness is located in northern Scotland.

2. *Explain why some say that the Loch Ness Monster sightings date back at least 1,500 years.* Carvings done by ancient people of the Scottish Highlands show a giant aquatic creature.

3. *Describe the reported sighting of Nessie in 1933.* Mr. and Mrs. John Mackay reported that they had seen "an enormous animal rolling and plunging on the surface" of Loch Ness. They described the animal as a monster about 40 to 50 feet long with two humps, a tail, and a snakelike head.

4. *How have sightings of Nessie helped the area?* Nessie has increased the tourist trade.

5. *Tell about the fake photograph that was circulated of Nessie.* After being ridiculed for hunting the Loch Ness Monster, Marmaduke Wetherell, with the help of his son-in-law, created a fake photo of Nessie. The photo was staged by making a clay model of Nessie and placing it in water.

6. *How were the credible photographs taken?* Scientists used sonar and underwater cameras equipped with high-powered lights to try to capture the creature photographically. The high-powered lights were necessary because the deep waters are so dark.

7. *What do some scientists say about Nessie being a plesiosaur?* The plesiosaur lived about 165 million years ago. Because the plesiosaur became extinct around 65 million years ago, Nessie is probably not a plesiosaur. They say that if it were a plesiosaur, like other reptiles it would have to emerge from the water more frequently in order to breathe.

8. *Why do some think Nessie might be an underwater wave?* Because the lake is located on a fault line, seismic rumblings sometimes occur. These can create rolling waves, which might resemble a large underwater animal.

9. *Explain the importance of the fact that at one time all the lakes in the area might have been connected?* Scientists believe that at one time the chain of lakes were connected by underground caves. Nessie might have become trapped in the lake when the underwater caves collapsed.

10. *According to some zoologists, what animal might be a possible explanation for Nessie?* Some zoologists think that Nessie is probably a Baltic sturgeon, a primitive fish that can grow up to 9 feet in length and can weigh as much as 450 pounds!

The Loch Ness Monster
CREATIVE QUESTIONS

1. Which theory about Nessie sounds most likely to you? Give reasons to support your answer.

_____

_____

_____

2. Why might it have been important enough to the ancient people of Scotland to leave carvings of a giant aquatic creature?

_____

_____

_____

3. Suppose you had the opportunity to visit Loch Ness. What would you expect to see? Why do you think this?

_____

_____

_____

4. What might happen to the Loch Ness area if the Nessie enigma were proven just a myth?

_____

_____

_____

5. Which do you think is more likely, that Nessie is a plesiosaur or that Nessie is a Baltic sturgeon? Explain your answer.

_____

_____

_____

6. Do you think Wetherell was right in faking the photo of the Loch Ness Monster? Why or why not?

_____

_____

_____

7. How might you prove or disprove the existence of the Loch Ness Monster?

_____

_____

_____

8. Suppose the underwater cave system had not collapsed. What changes do you think might be seen in the lakes?

_____

_____

_____

9. What reasons would make scientists believe that the Loch Ness would not support a group of plesiosaurs?

_____

_____

_____

10. Suppose you were in a tourist boat in Loch Ness and Nessie suddenly appeared. How would you react? Explain your answer.

_____

_____

_____

Learning Center Activities
SUBJECT: The Loch Ness Monster

Name: _____

#1 **Write a story about the Loch Ness Monster.**	**#2** **Write a poem about the Loch Ness Monster.**
#3 **Create a travel brochure that would attract tourists to the Loch Ness area.**	**#4** **Create a learning center with at least 3 activities that would teach about Scotland and the Loch Ness Monster.**
#5 **Research the ancient people of the Scottish Highlands. Teach a lesson to the class about your findings.**	**#6** **Research the theories about Nessie. Choose one and create a test to prove or disprove it.**

Choose three activities to complete. As you complete each activity, record the date of completion.

Activity # _____   Completed _____

Activity # _____   Completed _____

Activity # _____   Completed _____

THE BERMUDA TRIANGLE

As Christopher Columbus was plotting the ship's direction, the compass began to spin strangely. Columbus called the ship's navigator over so he could see how the compass was reacting. Suddenly a bright light appeared overhead. Columbus and everyone aboard looked up trying to understand what they were seeing.

Think of how Columbus must have felt not having the knowledge that we do today. The above re-creation came from details in Columbus's log about the strange happenings that occurred in what was called the Sargasso Sea. Columbus and other explorers dreaded sailing through the area. Many actually sailed out of their way to stay away from what is now referred to as the Bermuda Triangle. Columbus was luckier than many. He, his men, and the ship sailed on to their destination. Many who traveled in water vessels or planes have not escaped the clutches of the Bermuda Triangle.

Early recorded military disappearances began in 1918 with the *U.S.S. Cyclops*. This occurred during World War I when the *Cyclops* had been sent to Brazil as a refueling station for British ships in the south Atlantic. On February 16 the *Cyclops* left Rio de Janeiro and headed for Baltimore. Maryland. However, the captain decided to stop at Barbados along the way. The ship was in Barbados from March 3 to March 4. It then left the harbor and was never heard from again. The *Cyclops* and all 306 crew members disappeared!

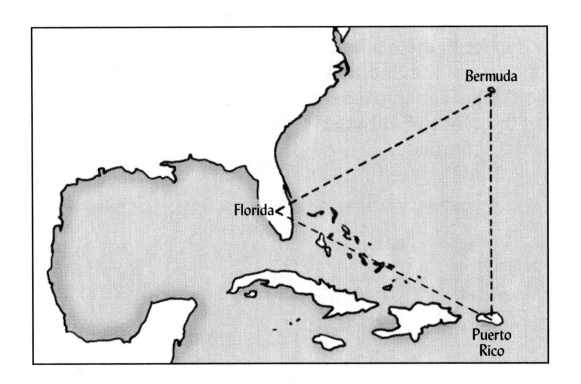

One of the most famous disappearances involving the Bermuda Triangle occurred on December 5, 1945, when five United States naval pilots and their planes mysteriously disappeared. Known as Flight 19, the pilots took off on a training flight from the U.S. Naval Station at Fort Lauderdale, Florida, around 2:10 p.m. The last communication heard by command headquarters from Flight 19 was an intercepted from the leader to one of the other pilots. At 4:00 p.m. the leader, who was the instructor, stated that he was unsure of their position. He also said that the planes' compasses were malfunctioning. That was the last contact anyone had with Flight 19. The coast guard and naval rescue boats searched for the five planes with no success. No remains were found of the aircraft or the pilots. The incident's cause was written as "an unexplained disappearance" rather than pilot error.

There have been many other reports of missing ships and planes. Some ships have been found floating, but without any passengers or crew. One ship was found that had food on the table and warm coffee in the cups, but no one was on board. To date there have been close to 200 aircraft and 1,000 water vessels that have disappeared in the area called the Bermuda Triangle. Searches of the underwater area have not revealed the wreckage of many of the missing vessels.

The so-called Bermuda Triangle is located off the southeastern Atlantic coast of the United States from Miami, Florida, southeast to Puerto Rico, northeast to Bermuda and back to Miami. It covers about 500,000 square miles. Though it is popularly called the Bermuda Triangle, it is not really triangular in shape, but rather trapezoidal. The United States Board of Geographic Names does not recognize the Bermuda Triangle as an official place, and the name cannot be found on any U.S. government-issued map. According to the US Navy, there is no such place as the Bermuda Triangle. Although the United States denies its existence, however, many other countries do show the area on nautical and aviation charts!

In the past the Bermuda Triangle has also been called, "The Devil's Triangle," "The Watery Triangle," "The Deadly Triangle," "The Sea of Doom," "The Graveyard of the Atlantic," "The Sargasso Graveyard," and other names that gives one a sense of fear. Many—from scientists to psychics to explorers—have tried to explain the strange happenings that occur in this area; however, none can pinpoint the reason for so many disappearances of sea- and aircraft and their passengers.

Scientists do agree that there are some different land formations on the ocean's floor and strange, unexplainable deviations that take place in the area. As with most enigmas, there are many theories that try to explain the causes. Some make sense and some are farfetched ideas; however, many agree that ships and planes do disappear in the Bermuda Triangle.

THEORIES

When trying to find an answer for strange occurrences, one must look at all the theories and find facts that will support the most plausible. The following are some of the theories about the Bermuda Triangle.

- Some feel that the lost civilization of Atlantis is located on the ocean floor in the Bermuda Triangle area. A well-known psychic, Edgar Cayce, claimed to have had some visions about Atlantis. He reported that it had modern-day technologies that included a death-ray weapon which was powered by energy crystals. Cayce said that Atlantis was destroyed by its own weapon. He theorized that because the energy crystals were so powerful, they retained that power.

- Natural weather phenomena have also been used to explain the sudden disappearance of vessels in the Bermuda Triangle. For instance, sudden storms or hurricanes can sink a sea craft or bring down an airplane.

- A strong ocean current, the Gulf Stream, runs through the Bermuda Triangle area. The current is very fast and turbulent. If a vessel sinks, proof of its existence can be quickly swept away by the Gulf Stream to other parts of the ocean where searchers would not look.

- Magnetic abnormalities have also been used to explain the Bermuda Triangle. Compasses used on ships and planes have been reported to spin crazily in the area. This may be due to the fluctuations of the Earth's magnetic field.

- An electronic fog has been reported to have caused the loss of direction with some craft. In 1970 Bruce Germon and his father were flying in a plane over the Bermuda Triangle when a strange cloud appeared. As they flew over it, the cloud seemed to expand and follow them, soon turning into a large tunnel-shaped area. Germon saw no way around the tunnel, so he flew into it. Once inside, the plane's instruments went crazy. They thought they would fly through it and find sunlit sky on the other side; instead they found a gray area with only about two miles of visibility. When Germon and his father finally flew clear of the fog, they noticed that their watches and the plane's instruments showed a loss of time. This led them to believe that the electronic fog created a time-travel effect.

- Blue holes are steep-walled, circular depressions on the ocean floor. Some people believe that the blue holes are linked to micro-wormholes that are thought to be transit points for UFOs that travel between dimensions. The blue holes might pull ships and planes down into them.

- Scientists are currently studying the possibility that exploding large pockets of methane gas might be the cause. The explosion would push the gas up to the ocean surface, creating a blowout. If a ship happened to be floating above the blowout, it might sink to the bottom. If a plane happened to be flying above a blowout, it could catch fire and crash. Methane-gas blowouts have been proven to be the cause of the sinking of several oil-drilling rigs.

- Pirates have also been discussed as a cause for ships disappearing. The history of pirates can be traced back hundreds of years. Pirates are still active on the high seas. They hijack both large and small craft. Smaller vessels are used for transporting drugs. Cargo transported by the larger ships is stolen and sold.

There have been many theories proposed to explain the Bermuda Triangle throughout history. As long as water craft, aircraft and their passengers continue to disappear, the Bermuda Triangle will remain an enigma.

The Bermuda Triangle
DISCUSSION QUESTIONS

1. Explain what problems Columbus had in the area known as the Bermuda Triangle.

_____

_____

_____

2. Describe the first recorded military disappearance of a vessel in the area known as the Bermuda Triangle.

_____

_____

_____

3. What has been described as the most famous disappearance and when did it take place?

_____

_____

_____

4. About how many planes and how many water craft are thought to have disappeared in the Bermuda Triangle?

_____

_____

_____

5. What is the location of the Bermuda Triangle?

_____

_____

_____

6. What is the official position of United States regarding the Bermuda Triangle?

_____

_____

_____

7. Explain how methane gas might cause a ship to disappear.

_____

_____

_____

8. What is the Gulf Stream? How might it affect the area?

_____

_____

_____

9. Which weather phenomena might be responsible for some of the disappearances?

_____

_____

_____

10. What role might pirates play in the disappearance of ships in the Bermuda Triangle?

_____

_____

_____

ANSWERS TO " THE BERMUDA TRIANGLE"
DISCUSSION QUESTIONS

1. *Explain what problems Columbus had in the area known as the Bermuda Triangle.* He reported his compass acting strangely and seeing a bright light overhead.

2. *Describe the first recorded military disappearance of a vessel in the area known as the Bermuda Triangle.* The *U.S.S. Cyclops* and its 306 passengers disappeared during World War I on the way from Brazil to Baltimore, Maryland, after stopping in Barbados.

3. *What was has been described as the most famous disappearance and when did it take place?* Flight 19 disappeared on December 5, 1945. Flight 19 included a group of five pilots and their planes on a routine training exercise.

4. *About how many planes and how many water craft are thought to have disappeared in the Bermuda Triangle?* About 200 planes and 1,000 water craft have been reported to have disappeared.

5. *What is the location of the Bermuda Triangle?* The Bermuda Triangle is located off the southeastern Atlantic coast of the United States.

6. *What is the official position of United States regarding the Bermuda Triangle?* The United States government does not recognize that there is such a place and does not include it on any maps. The U.S. navy denies that the Bermuda Triangle really exists.

7. *Explain how methane gas might cause a ship to disappear?* Methane gas can create an underwater explosion that reaches the surface sinking anything above it.

8. *What is the Gulf Stream? How might it affect the area?* The current is very fast and turbulent. If a vessel sinks, proof of its existence can be quickly swept away by the Gulf Stream to other parts of the ocean where searchers would not look.

9. *Which natural weather phenomena might be responsible for some of the disappearances?* Natural weather causes might include sudden storms, hurricanes, or strong winds.

10. *What role might pirates play in the disappearance ships in the Bermuda Triangle?* Pirates might hijack ships and use them for drug transportation or to steal cargo.

The Bermuda Triangle
CREATIVE QUESTIONS

1. What do you think might have happened to Flight 19? Give reasons to support your answer.

_____

_____

_____

2. Evaluate the theory regarding energy crystals left over from the lost civilization of Atlantis.

_____

_____

_____

3. What do you think might have happened to the missing passengers on the ship that was found in the Bermuda Triangle area?

_____

_____

_____

4. Do you think there could really be an electronic fog that instigates time travel? Why or why not?

_____

_____

_____

5. Do you think the Bermuda Triangle deserves its reputation? Why or why not?

_____

_____

_____

6. How might you handle the situation if your compass suddenly acted crazy while on a hiking trip? How would this experience be similar to that of the captain of a ship or the pilot of a plane if the same thing occurred?

_____

_____

_____

7. If given the opportunity, would you take a cruise on a ship traveling through the Bermuda Triangle? Why or why not?

_____

_____

_____

8. How do you feel about the official stand taken by the United States government regarding the Bermuda Triangle? Give reasons to support your answer.

_____

_____

_____

9. How might pirates benefit from the Bermuda Triangle's reputation?

_____

_____

_____

10. What do you think might be found in the blue holes? Explain your answer.

_____

_____

_____

Learning Center Activities
SUBJECT: The Bermuda Triangle

Name: _____

#1
Create an underwater city that might be found in the Bermuda Triangle area. Draw pictures of the city.

#2
Suppose you were on a ship that disappeared in the Bermuda Triangle and ended up in a different world. Write about your experience.

#3
Write a news report about the disappearance of a ship in the Bermuda Triangle.

#4
Create a board game about the Bermuda Triangle.

#5
Research one or two theories about the Bermuda Triangle and prepare a presentation to explain your findings to the class.

#6
Set up an experiment that would test one of the Bermuda Triangle theories. Keep a journal of the results.

Choose three activities to complete. As you complete each activity, record the date of completion.

Activity # _____   Completed _____

Activity # _____   Completed _____

Activity # _____   Completed _____

THE NAZCA LINES

Standing in the Nazca Desert you would probably not notice the enigma that surrounds you. If you flew over it and looked down, however, you would see strange shapes that seem to be etched into the land. Called geoglyphs, they include geometric shapes; plants; man-made objects such as yarn, looms, and clothing clasps; and more than 40 types of animals. There is even a drawing of what appears to be an ancient astronaut! Each is gigantic in size. For example, there is a bird with a 160-foot tail! More than 800 lines have been etched into the desert ground. They are mostly in an area of about 175 square miles of desert.

Experts believe that most of the Nazca Lines were created between 200 BCE and 600 CE, when the Nazca kingdom was flourishing. The figures still retain their shapes. One reason for their preservation is that the Nazca Desert is one of the driest places on earth. Also, because the ground is flat and stony, the lines are not in danger of being covered by dust or sand. Some shapes were made by using stones that outlined the shapes. Because of the size and details of the shapes, experts believe it took many hours to create the drawings. The lines also show how the creators' culture changed over time.

In 2006 a new figure was discovered by a group of Japanese researchers. It was the first new discovery since 1980. The newly discovered figure lies in an area not usually flown over by planes. It resembles an animal with horns and is thought to deal with fertility rituals.

The challenge for scientists is to discover how these mysterious figures were made at a time when modern technology, including planes and computers, were nonexistent. Because the Nazca people did create wondrous weavings, it is thought that they may have used a similar process to create the lines. Their designs would have been designed and then enlarged on a grid. Instead of being transferred to a loom, they would have been transferred to the land for etching out the designs.

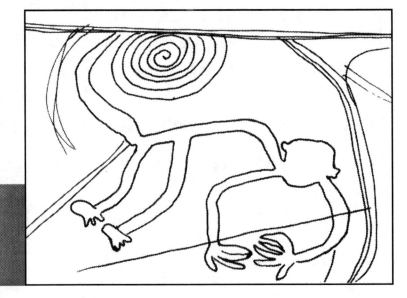

Scientists know that the lines were made by removing dark red stones and soil from the surface. The lighter soil which was underneath was exposed, thus causing the patterns to show up more distinctly. The creators then ran along the line paths to wear them down smoothly. This foot action caused them to show up even more. This process had to have taken many people and many hours of tedious work. It makes one wonder about the importance of the lines!

Recently a discovery was made that might help archaeologists solve the mystery of the purpose of the lines—the discovery of Cahuachi, the lost city of the culture that created the lines. Located south of the Nazca Lines, it was probably occupied from about 1 to about 450 CE. Then the city was mysteriously abandoned. Archaeologists found pieces of pottery in the area which provided important information about the Nazca people. The pottery carried some of the same figures as the lines. Discoveries of some burial sites with mummified bodies, well preserved due to the dry soil and climate, have provided new insight to how the lines may have been used. New knowledge about their ancient weaving techniques have also provided information about the different patterns of the lines.

At first archaeologists thought Cahuachi was a military stronghold; however, recent findings have caused them to change their beliefs. They now believe the city was a place for sacred ceremonies. Archaeologists think that Cahuachi was eventually destroyed as a result of natural disasters. Before it was abandoned, the people covered the city with pampa sand, leaving nothing to see but a mound.

Theories about the line builders and the purpose of the lines range from aliens creating lined landing strips for their ships to Indians creating ritual lines for worshiping their gods. Many feel the Nazca people did not have the technology to create the lines; however, we know that the Mayas, the Aztecs, the Incas, and ancient Egyptians were also very advanced for the period of time in which they lived. All of these Stone-Age cultures possessed the technology to build great pyramids and to create calendars, solar and religious, which were not known or understood by most cultures of the time period.

The Nazca Lines are of historical value because they help us understand cultures of the past. Unfortunately, these ancient treasures are slowly being destroyed by robbers, by tourists driving across them, and by companies that are providing the surrounding areas with energy sources. Archaeologists are fearful that many of the figures will be erased from the earth in the near future if nothing is done to protect them.

THEORIES

Many questions about the Nazca Lines continue to puzzle us. For example, why would the figures have been created when they can't really be enjoyed except by observing them high in the sky, impossible during that time period? Archaeologists and other scientists are challenged to discover the reason for their existence.

- Some of the figures resemble constellations. Some scientists believe the Nazca Lines were created as an astronomical calendar. They may have helped the people to locate the stars and planets and to plot the planet and star positions. The ancient astronomers may have left the line markings to note their discoveries.

- Another theory suggests that the lines were a landing strip used by ancient astronauts. This theory is supported by the fact that one of the figures resembles an astronaut.

- Some people think that the lines are actually paths to subterranean water. One scientist used rod dowsing to test the theory. A person holding a Y-shaped stick walks around; if the stick pulls down towards the ground, water is supposed to be present in that area. This method of searching for underground water has been used for thousands of years, but it has no scientific basis and is considered a type of divination.

- Some think that the lines were created and used for sacred ceremonies and rituals. They feel that the lines represent paths to the gods and that the lines were considered offerings to the gods for providing them with water to irrigate their fields.

- Some archaeologists have suggested that the lines are symbols of different clans that lived in the area.

- Others feel the creators of the lines were telling the story of creation through the figures etched in the ground.

- Although most archaeologists do not agree, some theorists think that the Maya traveled south to the Cahuachi/Nazca area in search of the sun.

There are many more theories that try to explain the lines' purpose. Those who support a certain theory seem to feel passionate about that theory. The Nazca Lines may always remain an enigma, but it is challenging to research and learn about the lines and the people who created them.

The Nazca Lines

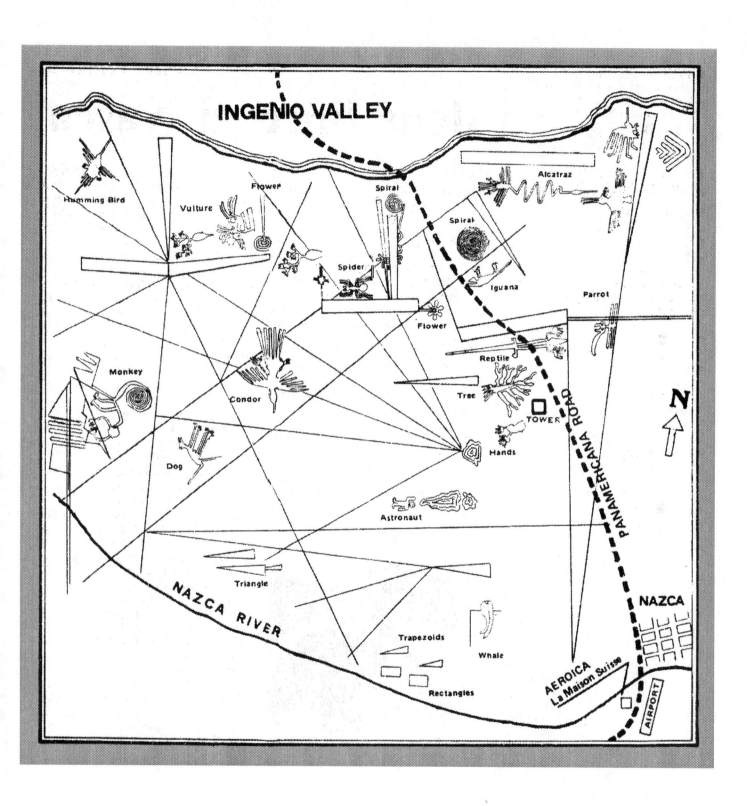

The Nazca Lines
DISCUSSION QUESTIONS

1. When were the Nazca lines created?

_____

_____

_____

2. Describe some of their shapes.

_____

_____

_____

3. What two factors have helped to preserve the lines?

_____

_____

_____

4. Describe the most recently discovered figure. Who discovered it?

_____

_____

_____

5. How do scientists think the lines were created?

_____

_____

_____

6. What discovery has allowed archaeologists to learn more about the Nazca people?

_____

_____

_____

7. What comparison causes archaeologists to believe that the creators of the lines might have had the technology necessary to create the lines?

_____

_____

_____

8. Upon what is the theory that the lines might have been used as a landing strip for ancient astronauts based?

_____

_____

_____

9. Name two theories that suggest people other than the Nazca created the lines.

_____

_____

_____

10. How might the lines have something to do with the stars and planets?

_____

_____

_____

ANSWERS TO "THE NAZCA LINES"
DISCUSSION QUESTIONS

1. *When were the Nazca lines created?* Most of the Nazca Lines were probably created between 200 BCE and 600 CE.

2. *Describe some of their shapes.* The shapes include geometric shapes; many types of animals and plants; and man-made objects such as yarn, looms, and clothing clasps. There is even a drawing of what appears to be an ancient astronaut! Each is gigantic in size.

3. *What two factors have helped to preserve the lines?* The reason for their preservation is that the Nazca Desert is one of the driest places on earth. Also, because the ground is flat and stony, the lines are not in danger of being covered by dust or sand.

4. *Describe the most recently discovered figure. Who discovered it?* The figure resembles an animal with horns and is thought to deal with fertility rituals. It was discovered by Japanese researchers.

5. *How do scientists think the lines were created?* The dark red stones and soil were removed, leaving the lighter soil. The lines were then run on by the builders to create a well-defined path.

6. *What discovery has allowed archaeologists to learn more about the Nazca people?* The discovery of Cahuachi, the lost Nazca city, has increased their understanding of the Nazca.

7. *What comparison causes archaeologists to believe that the creators of the lines might have had the technology necessary to create the lines?* They know that the Mayas, the Incas, the Aztecs, and the ancient Egyptians had the technology to build great structures even though they were of the Stone Age.

8. *Upon what is the theory that the lines might have been used as a landing strip for ancient astronauts based?* It is based on the fact that one of the figures resembles an astronaut.

9. *Name two theories that suggest people other than the Nazca created the lines.* One theory suggests they were created by aliens from another planet. Another suggests the Mayas created them. Neither is supported by archaeologists.

10. *How might the lines have something to do with the stars and planets?* Some of the figures resemble constellations. The Nazca Lines might have been created as an astronomical calendar which helped the people to locate the stars and planets and to plot their positions. The ancient astronomers might have left line markings to note their discoveries. Another theory suggests they were used to follow the sun's pattern.

The Nazca lines
CREATIVE QUESTIONS

1. One theory suggests that the lines were used in sacred ceremonies. What do you think some of those ceremonies might have been?

_____

_____

_____

2. Evaluate the importance of the discovery of Cahuachi.

_____

_____

_____

3. In your opinion, what other discoveries from ancient civilizations have helped us understand the past?

_____

_____

_____

4. Which theory do you support as the most likely reason for the lines? Explain.

_____

_____

_____

5. Why, do you think, was the city of Cahuachi covered when abandoned?

_____

_____

_____

6. Why, do you think, was the city abandoned and not rebuilt?

_____

_____

_____

7. Do you agree with the theory that aliens from another planet might have created the lines? Why or why not?

_____

_____

_____

8. Suppose you were asked to analyze one of the figures. Which one would you choose and what would you say about it?

_____

_____

_____

9. How do you think the Nazca burial sites might have helped archaeologists to understand the culture better?

_____

_____

_____

10. The Nazca Lines are being destroyed by the need for modern technology in the area. What would you suggest to help in the preservation of the Nazca Lines?

_____

_____

_____

Learning Center Activities
SUBJECT: The Nazca Lines

Name: _____

#1 Write a poem about the Nazca Lines.	**#2** Using pebbles, glue them onto poster board in the form of one of the figures found among the Nazca Lines.
#3 Create a grid and draw a shape. Now use another grid to draw the same shape three times as large. Write about the experience.	**#4** Pretend to discover a new figure. Draw its shape and write a description of the discovery for a scientific magazine. Remember that it is a gigantic figure.
#5 Research the Nazca people. Present your findings to the class as a lesson on the ancient civilization.	**#6** Choose two theories and further research them. Which do you feel is more reasonable? Give an explanation for your answer.

Choose three activities to complete. As you complete each activity, record the date of completion.

Activity # _____   Completed _____

Activity # _____   Completed _____

Activity # _____   Completed _____

Learning Center Activities
PLANNING SHEET

NAME: _____

EXPLORER: _____

SUMMARY OF ACTIVITY	PRODUCT	MATERIALS NEEDED

Learning Center Activities

SUBJECT: _____

Name: _____

#1	**#2**
#3	**#4**
#5	**#6**

Choose three activities to complete. As you complete each activity, record the date of completion.

Activity # _____   Completed _____

Activity # _____   Completed _____

Activity # _____   Completed _____

RESEARCH UNIT

Research Unit Directions

Choose an enigma to research.

Sources

Choose two or three resources to use for your research. One may be an internet source.

Bloom Questions

Read about Bloom's Taxonomy on pages 92–95. Using the template, write a Bloom question from each level based regarding your insect to help guide you in your research. When you have completed the Bloom questions, you will be ready to research so you can answer your Bloom questions.

Note Cards

Not all information in your resources will be important for your research. You will break the information down into categories, or topics, and record the important information onto note cards. This is a good way to get organized.

Use a different color card for each source. (If you don't have colored cards, use a sticker or a dot. Put the bibliographic information on the first card of each color. Each card within the color-coded set will pertain to the same category, or topic. Write the category at the top if each card. (See page 96.) As you do your research, add information to your note cards. Read about summarizing and plagiarism on page 97.

Bibliography

Create a bibliography of the sources you have used. (See pages 98–100.)

Graphic Organizer and Outline

After completing your research, use your note cards to organize the information into a graphic organizer. (See pages 101–102.)

Once the graphic organizer is finished, you may want to convert it to an outline. (See page 103.)

Product

You are now ready to choose a product that will reflect your research. (See pages 104–105.) Fill out a product proposal using the form on page 106 to help you plan your product. When finished, evaluate the project by using the product evaluation form on page 107.

Presentation

You are now ready to give your presentation. See pages 108-109.

Levels of Bloom's Taxonomy

Benjamin Bloom divided educational questions into six main categories; they are knowledge, comprehension, application, analysis, synthesis and evaluation. The last four levels promote critical and creative thinking.

Level	_Skill Involved_
Knowledge:	simple recall
Comprehension:	understanding of the material
Application:	applying learned information to a new situation
Analysis:	the breaking down of learned knowledge into small parts
Synthesis:	creating something new and original from the acquired knowledge
Evaluation:	making a judgment and backing it up

Question Cues

The following verbs can help in writing Bloom questions.

Knowledge: list, know, define, relate, repeat, recall, specify, tell, name

Comprehension: recognize, restate, explain, describe, summarize, express, review, discuss, identify, locate, report, retell

Application: demonstrate, interview, simulate, dramatize, experiment, show, use, employ, operate, exhibit, apply, calculate, solve, illustrate

Analysis: compare, examine, categorize, group, test, inventory, probe, analyze, discover, arrange, organize, contrast, classify, survey

Synthesis: plan, develop, invent, predict, propose, produce, arrange, formulate, construct, incorporate, originate, create, prepare, design, set up

Evaluation: value, recommend, evaluate, criticize, estimate, decide, conclude, predict, judge, compare, rate, measure, select, infer

Bloom Questions

Knowledge

1. List the parts of _____.
2. Define how to _____.
3. What does _____ mean?

Comprehension

1. Describe how to _____.
2. Explain how _____ happened.
3. Locate where _____ is found.

Application

1. Demonstrate how to _____.
2. Tell how to operate a _____.
3. Dramatize how _____ is different today.

Analysis

1. Compare and contrast _____ and _____.
2. How would you test _____?
3. Organize _____ and test it.

Synthesis

1. Plan a new way to _____.
2. Create a new _____. Explain it.
3. Design a way to _____.

Evaluation

1. Judge the usefulness of _____.
2. Predict how _____ may change _____.
3. Recommend _____ to someone.

Note Cards and Organization

Use color-coded note cards. (If colored cards are not available, use markers to put colored dots in the corner.) Put all the information from one source on cards of the same color. For example, all pink cards may refer to a certain book; all blue cards may come from an internet source; all white cards come from a magazine source; etc.

Make sure the first card of a color has the resource information. (See card No. 1.) Each note card should have a title or category describing what that card is about. (See Card No. 2.)

Card No. 1

Jones, Sean. _Those Mysterious Lights._ New York: ABC Publishing, 2001.

Card No. 2

Marfa

western Texas

small town

outskirts of Big Bend National Park

sparsely populated region

Summarizing

To **summarize** is to pick out the important points of information. You then write (or say) them in a few words.

Original Paragraph:

On the outskirts of Big Bend National Park in West Texas lays the small, very ordinary town of Marfa. Located in one of the most sparsely populated regions of Texas, the area is home to many legends and unexplained happenings. What makes Marfa even mentionable are the strange dancing lights that have been observed since the early eighteen hundreds. Marfa is the home to the greatest unexplainable mystery in Texas…the Marfa Lights.

Summary for Note Card: Location

western Texas
small town
outskirts of Big Bend National Park
sparsely populated region

Plagiarism

When someone writes a report and uses the exact words from the author of the source, it is called plagiarism. The following is an example of plagiarism. The student used almost the same words as the author.

On the outskirts of Big Bend National Park in West Texas lays a small, ordinary town of Marfa. In one of the most sparsely populated regions of Texas, the area is home to many legends and unexplained happenings. What makes Marfa notable are the strange dancing lights that have been observed since the early eighteen hundreds. Marfa is the home to one of the greatest unexplainable mysteries in Texas…the Marfa Lights.

Here is the same information put into the student's own words. This is not plagiarism:

A small town located in a rural area of West Texas near Big Bend National Park has gained notoriety from some unexplained strange lights that seem to appear at night. Many legends exist about the famous Marfa Lights, which have been reported since the early eighteen hundreds.

When you summarize the information in your own words, it is easier to avoid plagiarism.

About Bibliographies

A **bibliography** is a list of books and other sources of information. There are two main reasons to have a bibliography. First of all, it shows the research an author has done in preparing the work. It also tells readers where they can look if they want more information on the subject.

Each entry includes important information:

- Title of the Book

- Author's Name

- Name of Publisher

- Copyright Date

Entries are listed in alphabetical order. Alphabetical order is based on the first important word in the entry. Usually, that will be the author's last name. If an entry begins with a title, do not use the words "A," "An," or "The" to put the entries in order.

Bibliographies should be easy to read. Put a line space between each entry. Also, indent all lines in an entry except the first.

General Rules

Begin each entry at the left margin.

Indent all lines of an entry except the first.

Authors' names are written last name first.

If there are more than one author, write them in the same order as on the title page.

Alphabetize by the first important word in the entry.
   (Do not use "A," "An," or "The.")

Book and magazine titles should be printed in italics or underlined.

Tiles of articles in magazines are put in quotation marks.

Each entry should end with a period.

Skip a line between each entry.

Bibliography Formats

Follow the appropriate format for each type of resource. Be sure to notice the punctuation as well as the order of the information.

NOTE: If typed or handwritten, titles may be underlined instead of being done in italics. When no author is given, start with the name of the article.

Book Written by One Author:

Author's Last Name, Author's First Name. *Title of Book.* City Where Published: Publisher, Copyright / Publication Date.

Book Written by More Than One Author:

1st Author's Last Name, 1st Author's First Name, and 2nd Author's First and Last Name. (The rest is the same.)

If the same author has written more than one of the books, you may use a dash instead of the name. Alphabetize by the book title.

Encyclopedias and Other Reference Books:

Author's Last Name, Author's First Name (If known). "Title of Article." *Title of Reference Book.* Year of the Edition Used.

If you use an on-line encyclopedia, add the date you visited the site.

Magazines:

Author's Last Name, Author's First Name (If known). "Title of Article." *Magazine Name.* Date on Magazine: page(s).

World Wide Web:

Author's Last Name, Author's First Name (If known). "Title of Article." *Title of Work* (if there is one). Date you visited the site. <complete http address>.

Personal Interview:

Last Name, First Name. Personal Interview. Date Interviewed.

Graphic Organizers

A good tool to help you organize your notes is a graphic organizer. No matter what the pattern, a graphic organizer helps you to divide the topic into categories and to summarize the important information. You can use the graphic organizer as a guide when you write your report.

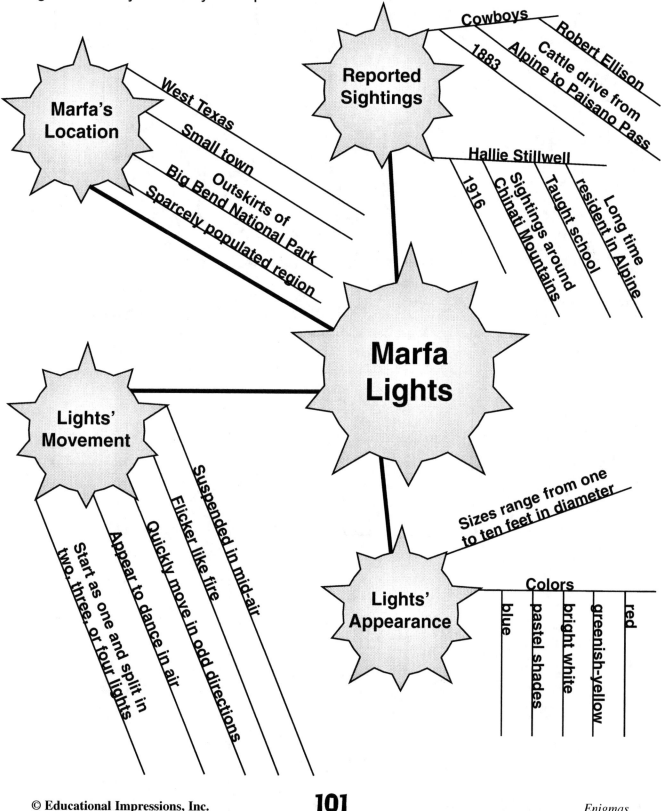

Other Formats of Graphic Organizers

Marfa Lights

I. Marfa's Location

    A. West Texas

    B. Small town

    C. Outskirts of Big Bend National Park

    D. Sparsely populated region

II. Reported Sightings

    A. Cowboys

        1. Robert Ellison

        2. cattle drive from Alpine to Paisano Pass

        3. 1883

    B. Hallie Stillwell

        1. long time resident in Alpine

        2. taught school

        3. sightings around Chinati Mountains

        4. 1916

III. Lights' Appearance

    A. Sizes range from one to ten feet in diameter

    B. Colors

        1. red

        2. greenish-yellow

        3. bright white

        4. pastel shades

        5. blue

IV. Lights' Movement

    A. Suspended in mid-air

    B. Flicker like fire

    C. Quickly move in odd directions

    D. Appear to dance in air

    E. Start as one and split into two, three, or four lights

Steps to Completing a Research Project

_____ 1. **Choose a topic.**

_____ 2. **Create a journal to keep up with the research process.**

_____ 3. **Collect data or research.**

      A. Use various sources as guides of where to find data.

          1. encyclopedias

          2. books

          3. magazines

          4. internet

      B. Cite the source information on the first card of each color. All information on the same color cards should belong to the same source.

      C. Decide on the categories and label the note cards. Put information about only one category on a note card. See the example on Note Cards and Organization.

_____ 4. **Develop a set of Bloom questions at each level for your topic.**

      (See Bloom section for examples.)

      A. Place each question on a separate note card.

      B. Using the collected data, answer the Bloom questions.

_____ 5. **Organize data.**

      A. Organize the cards into categories.

      B. Use the outline form to record the data retrieved from your cards.

_____ 6. **Write the paper.**

      A. Write a topic sentence.

      B. Using the outline, write the body of the paper.

      C. Have a closing sentence.

      D. Proofread and edit your paper.

      E. Have your teacher edit the paper.

      F. Write the final paper.

      G. Create a cover sheet.

_____ 7. **Create a product.**

      A. Use the Product Ideas sheet to choose a product.

      B. Use the Product Proposal sheet to plan your product.

      C. Develop the product.

      D. Evaluate the product by using the Product Evaluation form.

_____ 8. **Present your product orally.**

      A. Prepare an oral presentation for your paper and product.

      B. Have at least one visual to use in the presentation.

      C. Give the presentation to your class.

Product Ideas

diary

collection

puzzle

scrapbook

cartoon

invention

play

report

model

game

photograph display

teach a lesson

want ad

TV commercial

new theory

overhead transparency

display

story

brochure

mural

greeting card

diagram

speech

book cover

audio tape

advertisement

poem

radio show

graph

magazine article

diorama

map

pop-up book

sculpture

new product

skit

puppet show

secret code

newspaper article

flip book

time line

Product Proposal

Name of Product: _____

Supplies needed to make the product:

_____   _____

_____   _____

_____   _____

_____   _____

_____

Steps needed to make the product:

1. _____

2. _____

3. _____

4. _____

5. _____

6. _____

Did you have any problems?

_____

_____

_____

What could you do differently to make the product better?

_____

_____

_____

Product Evaluation

Are you pleased with your product? Why or why not?

_____

_____

_____

Do you think your product reflects your research? How?

_____

_____

_____

_____

If you scored your product, 1 being the lowest and 10 being the highest, what score would you give it? Circle one.

1   2   3   4   5   6   7   8   9   10

Give some reasons why you scored your product as you did.

_____

_____

_____

Did you enjoy making your product? Why or why not?

_____

_____

_____

Presentation Guidelines

Organize your presentation using the following outline. No matter what product you choose, you will have to present your information orally to the class. Use notes to help you present your research and your product.

I. Introduction

    A. Include a topic sentence.

    B. Be sure to grab your audience.

II. Body

    A. This will be the major part of the presentation of your product.

    B. Include important information.

    C. Know your information so that you refer to your notes as little as possible.

    D. Show any visuals you have included.

III. Conclusion

    A. Summarize your presentation in one or two sentences.

    B. Do not include any new material.

    C. Ask for questions.

    D. Answer the questions to the best of your ability.

Oral Presentation Tips

1. Know your topic and material well.

2. Be organized. Have your materials and information ready to use in your presentation.

3. Practice your presentation:

   • Do not read your presentation.

   • Give your presentation to anyone who will listen. Practice with your parents, your siblings, even your pets. The more often you give the presentation, the better and more comfortable you will become.

4. Make good eye contact with your audience.

5. Stand up straight, move a little, and don't stand in a frozen stance.

6. Use an oral presentation format:

   • Introduce your topic.

   • Explain each point you are trying to make.

   • Summarize your presentation with one or two sentences.

   • Ask if there are any questions.

7. Never turn your back on the audience.

8. Make sure your audience can hear you clearly.

   • Speak slowly so everyone can understand you.

Bibliography

Burl, Aubrey. *Stonehenge.* New York: Carroll & Graf Publishers, 2006.

Carlile, Vowery. *Ready to Research...Ancient Civilizations.* Hawthorne, NJ: Educational Impressions, Inc., 2006.

Johnson, Anthony. *Solving Stonehenge: The New Key to an Ancient Enigma.* High Holborn, London: Thames & Hudson Ltd, 2008.

Joseph, Frank. *The Destruction of Atlantis.* Rochester, Vermont: Bear & Company, 2002.

Hadingham, Evan. *Lines to the Mountain Gods: Nazca and the Mysteries of Peru.* Norman, Oklahoma: University of Oklahoma Press, 1988.

Plato. *Timaeus and Critias,* trans. Desmond Lee. London: Penguin Classics, 1977.

Simon, Seymour. *Pyramids & Mummies.* San Francisco, CA: Chronicle Books LLC, 2003.

Wassynger, Akamine Ruth. *Ancient Egypt.* New York: Scholastic Professional Books, 1996.

Web Sites

Hart, Will & Robert Berringer. "Ancient Civilizations: Six Great Enigmas." December 12, 2008. http://www.newdawnmagazine.com/Articles/Ancient_Civilisations_Six_Great_Enigmas....

"Atlantis" January 2, 2009. http://www.activemind.com/Mysterious/Topics/Atlantis

Chorvinsky, Mark. "Nessie, The Loch Ness Monster" January 20, 2009. http://www.strangemag.com/nessie.home.html

"Earth Mysteries Stonehenge." January 3, 2009. http://witcombe.sbc.edu/earthmysteries/EMStonehenge.html

"Egypt Secrets of an Ancient World." December 10, 2008. http://www.nationalgeographic.com/pyramids/khufu.html

"First English Settlement in the New World." January 19, 2009. http://statelibrary.dcr.state.nc.us/nc/ncsites/english2.htm

Hause, Eric. "The Lost Colony." December 10, 2008. http://www.coastalguide.com/packet/lostcolony-croatan.shtml

Lane, Ralph. "The Colony At Roanoke." December 10, 2008. http://www.nationalcenter.org/ColonyofRoanoke.html

"Loch Ness 'Monster'." January 20, 2009. http://skepdic.com/nessie.html

"Loch Ness Monster." January 20, 2009. http://www.crystalinks.com/loch_ness.html

"Lost Continent of Atlantis: Myth or Reality." January 2, 2009. http://atlantis.haktanir.org

"Nazca Lines." January 28, 2009. http://skepdic.com/nazca.html

"Nazca Lines and Culture." January 28, 2009. http://www.crystalinks.com/nasca.html

Obringer, Lee Ann. "How the Bermuda Triangle Works." January 28, 2009. http://science.howstuffworks.com/bermuda-triangle1.htm

"Stonehenge." January 4, 2009. http://en.wikipedia.org/wiki/Stonehenge

"The Loss of Flight 19." January 25, 2008. http://www.history.navy.mil/faqs/faq15-1.htm

"Texas Performance Standards Project." December 15, 2008. http://texaspsp.org

"The Bermuda Triangle." The History Channel, January 25, 2009.

"The Lost Colony of Roanoke, 1588." December 10, 2008. http://theshadowlands.net/roanoke.htm

"Theories About The Nazca Lines." January 28, 2009. http://www.world-mysteries.com/mpl_1_2.htm

Winston, Alan. "The Labors of Pyramid Building." December 12, 2008. http://www.touregypt.net/featurestories/pyramidworkforce.htm